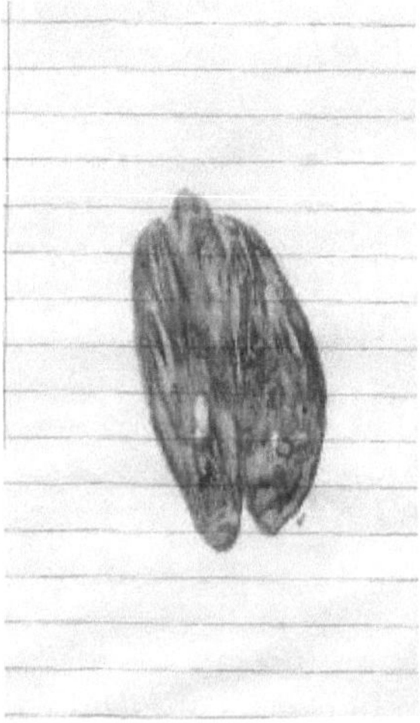

She Sings Unto The Gods Like A sweet Sparrow at Dusk!

Surreal Secret Two

Ron Koppelberger Jr.

***

Websites
Wolffray.blogspot.com
Farthermostdream.blogspot.com
Snakefuss.blogspot.com
Mirageinblame.blogspot.com
Ethrealsouls.blogspot.com
Horrorrush.blogspot.com
Ravenswont.blogspot.com

<u>Welcome</u>

I want this to be an ethereal experience for those interested in surreal artwork, the artwork of dreams, secret revelation and strange illusion. As with the other books I hope you find something worth remembering or noting in the compilation.....if you do find something here worth contemplating then I have accomplished my goal. I hope you enjoy the following presentation and as always dreams will be served after the show.

Ron Koppelberger Jr. Jan. 2013

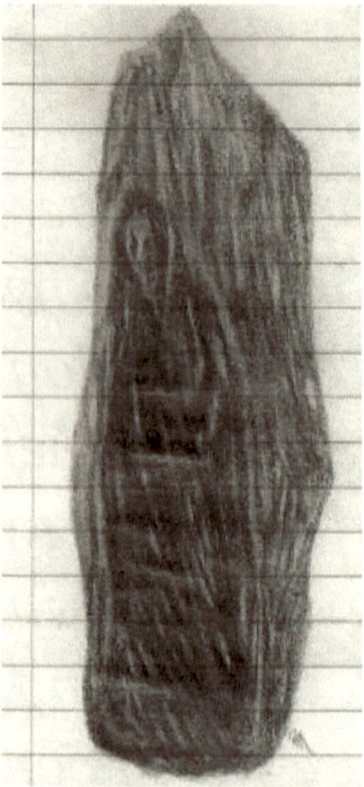

Image Of Doom

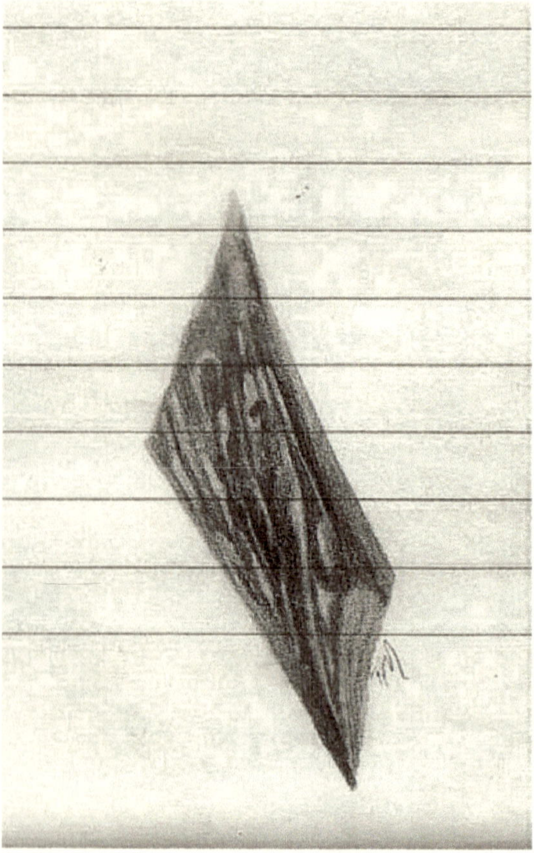

Shy Hands

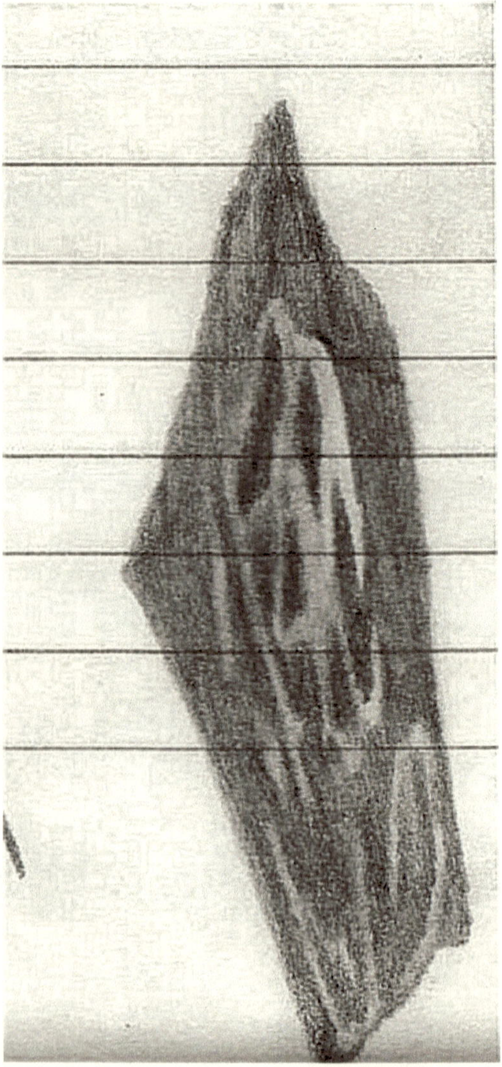

Skeleton Scream

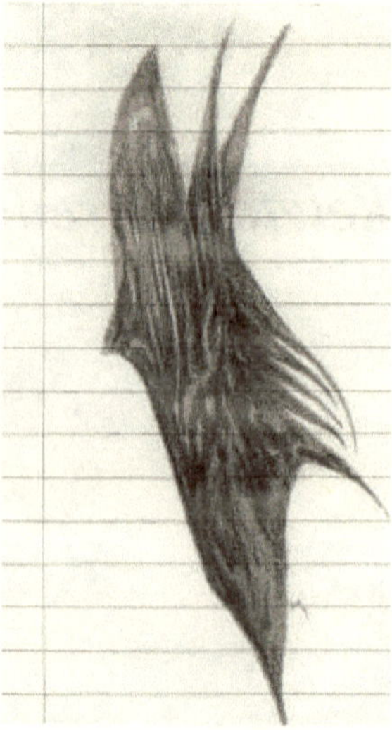

Venus Fly Trap

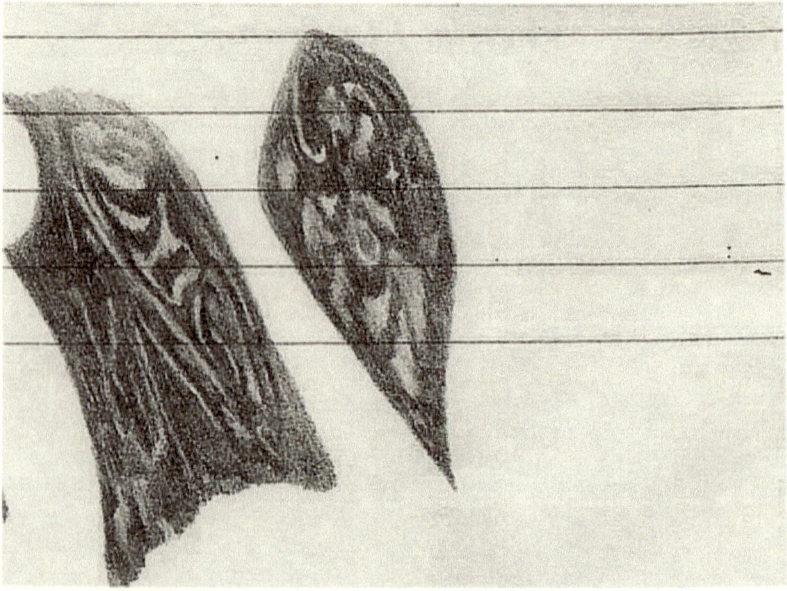

Sage Art

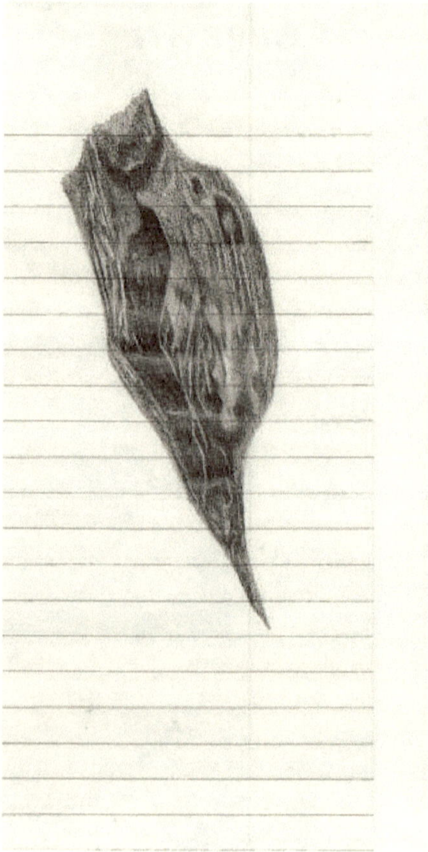

Dark Spirit

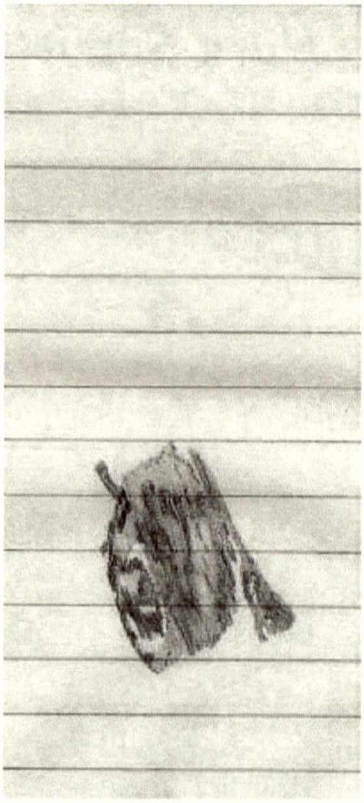

Zombie

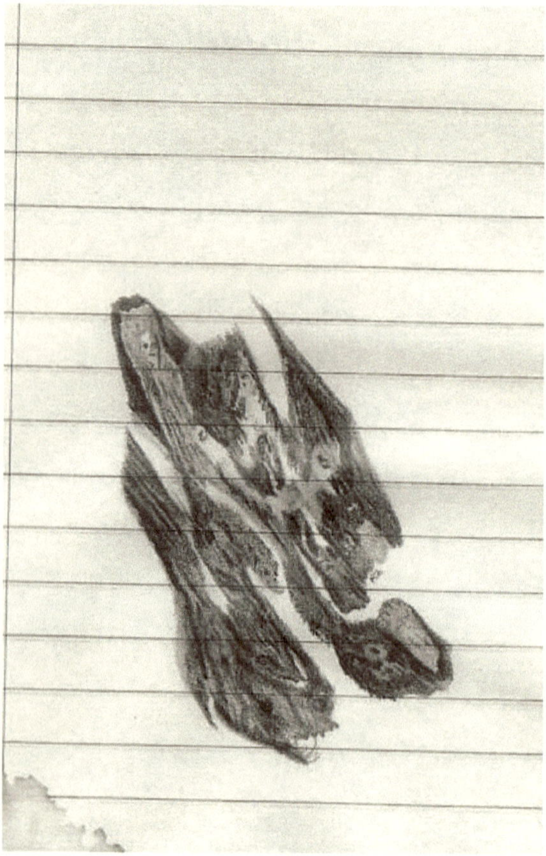

Dreams of Err

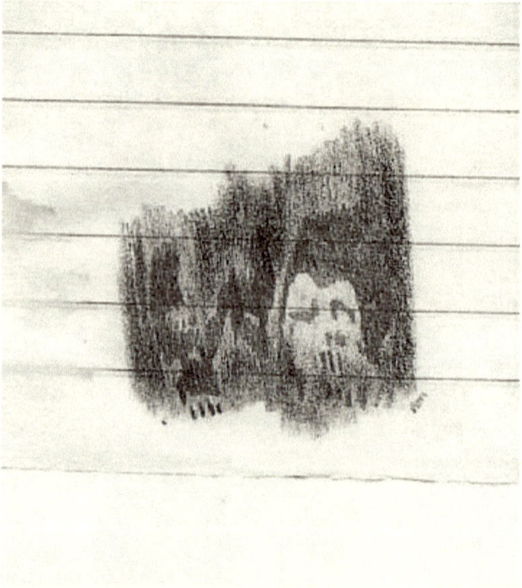

Black and White

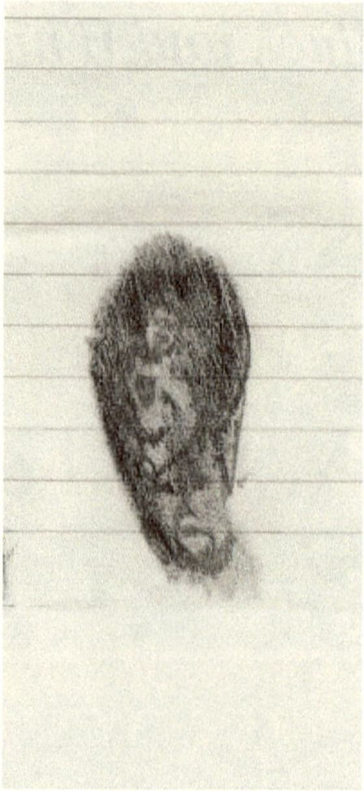

Twins

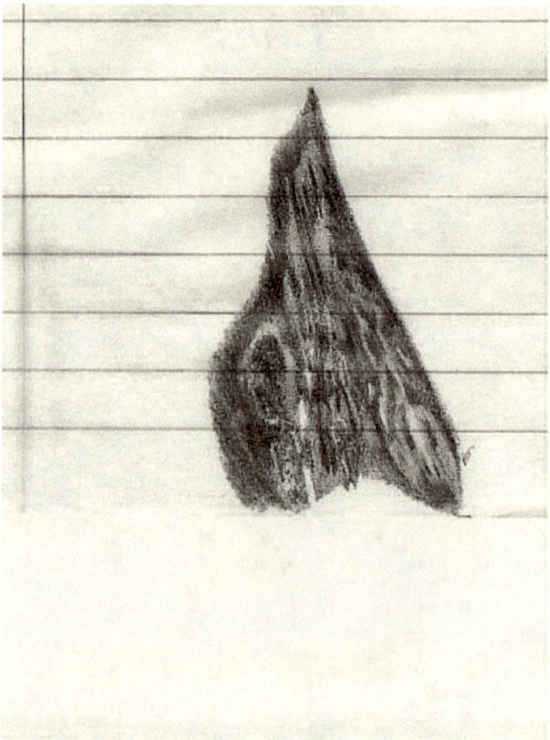

Bedraggled

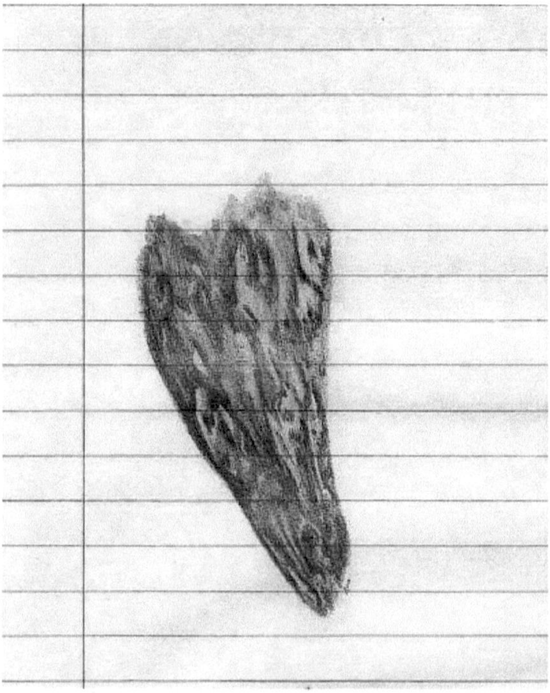

She Sings

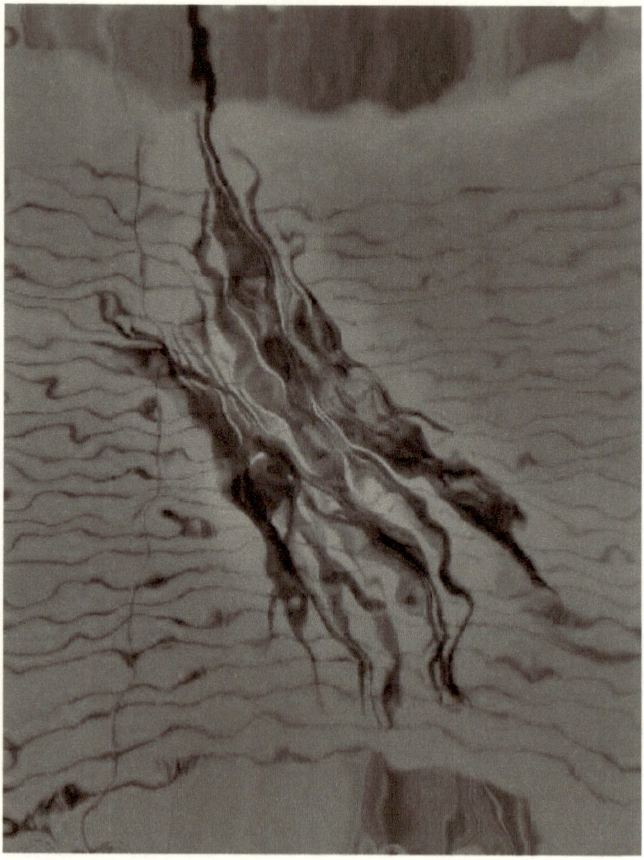

Sting Ray In Glass

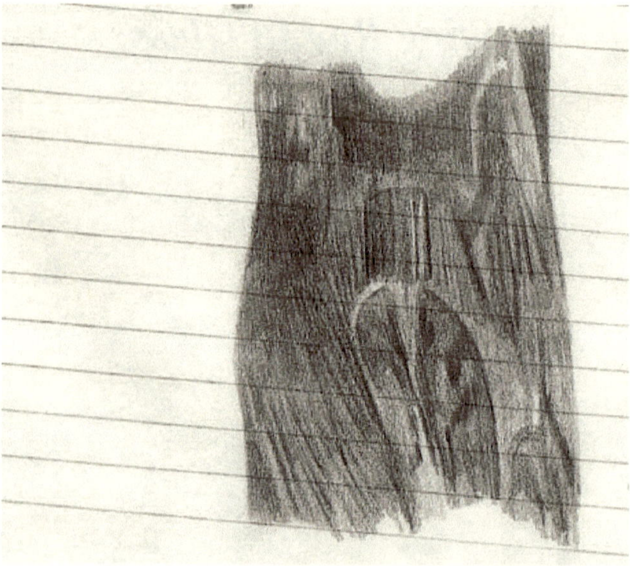

Man In A Cube

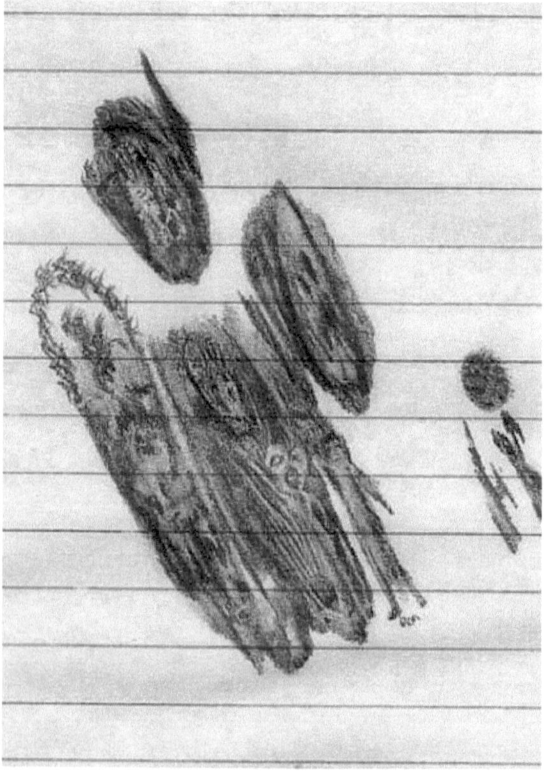

Religions

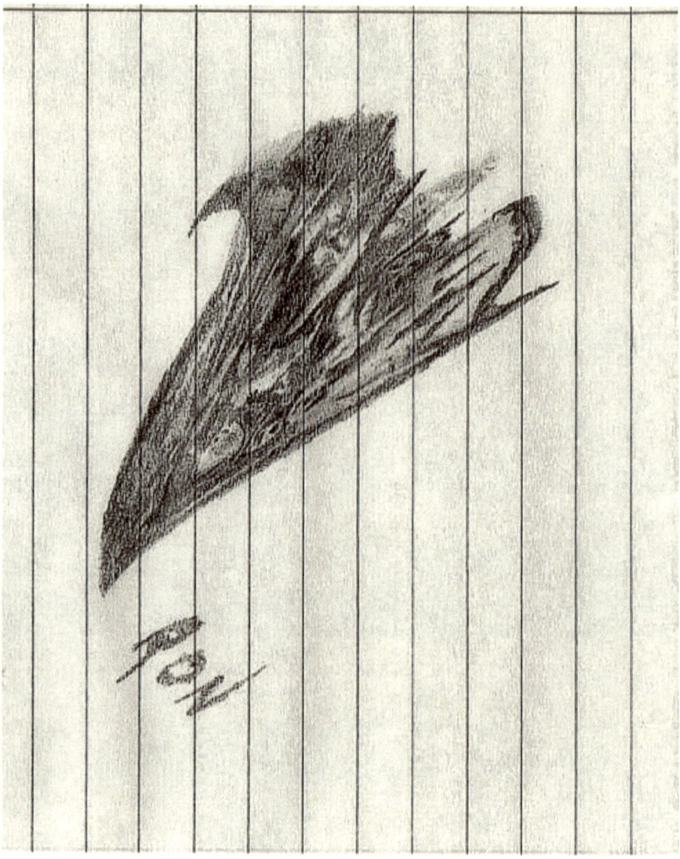

Parchment Secret

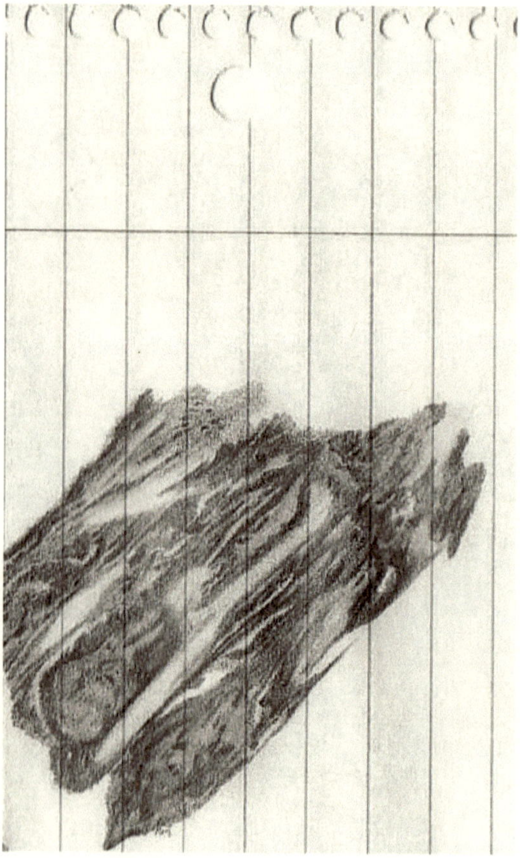

The Vulture

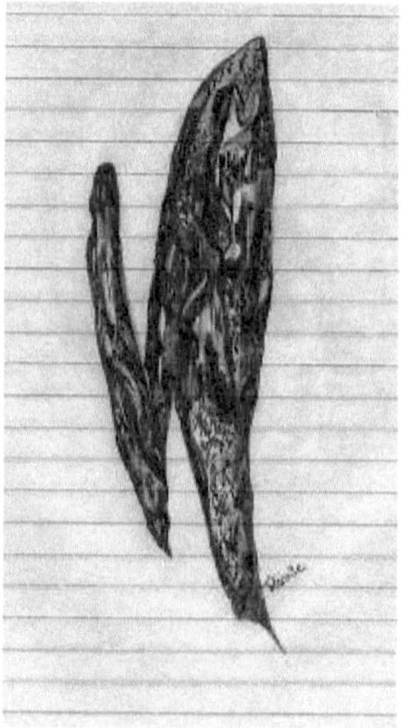

Barbed Wire

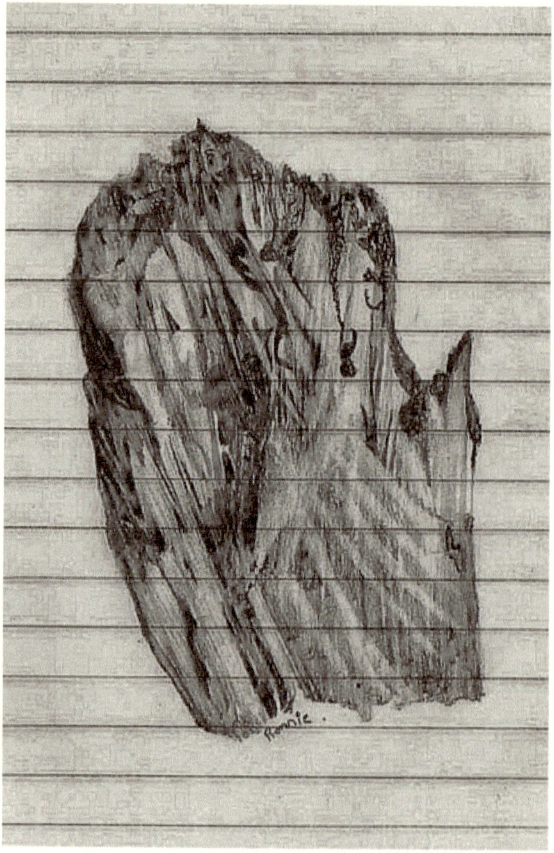

Halloween Preistess

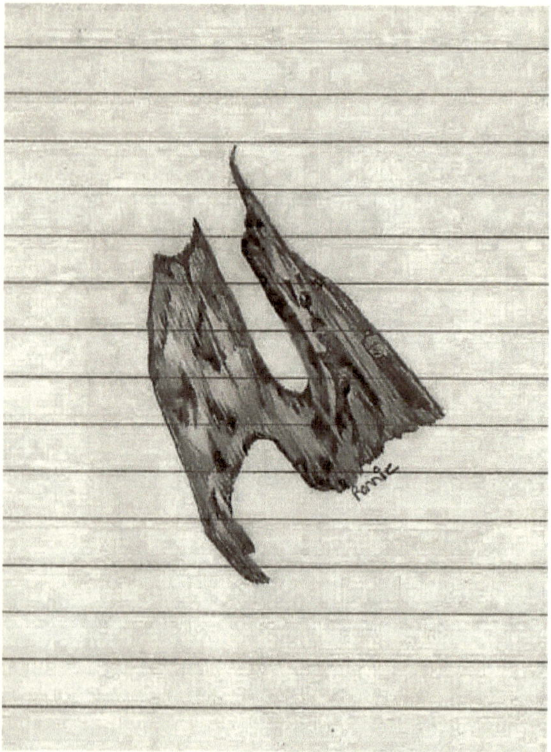

Through The Door To Forever

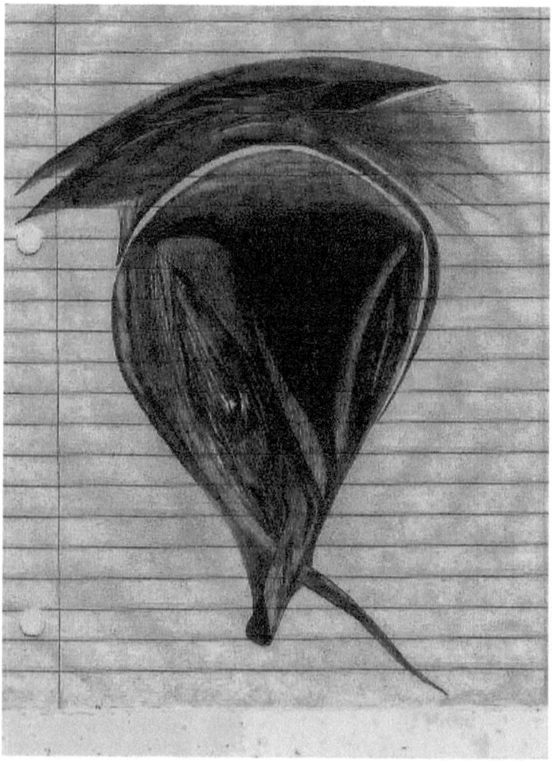

An Angel At Nights Reflection

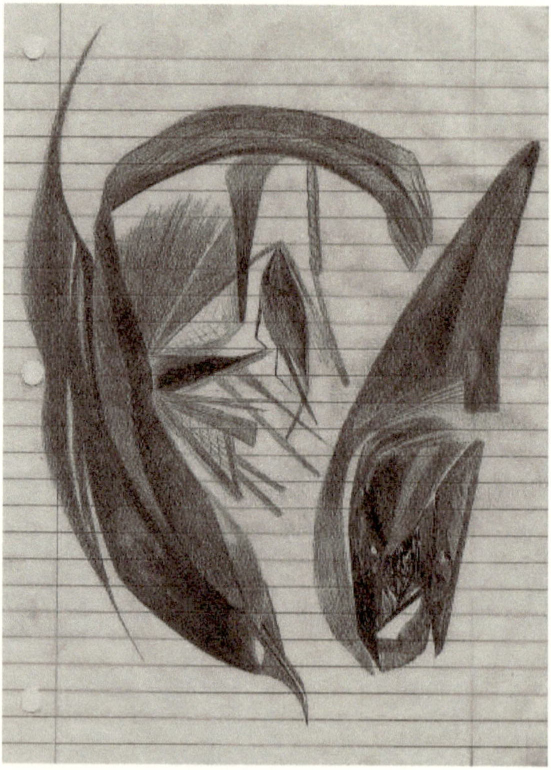

A Cricket

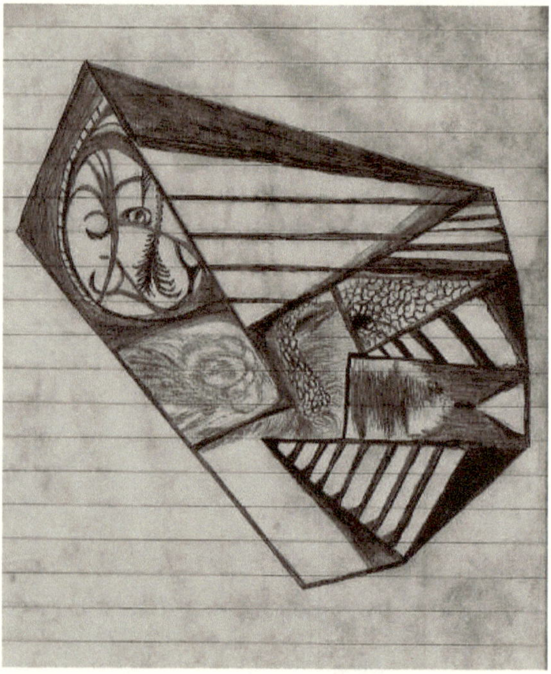

Different Paths

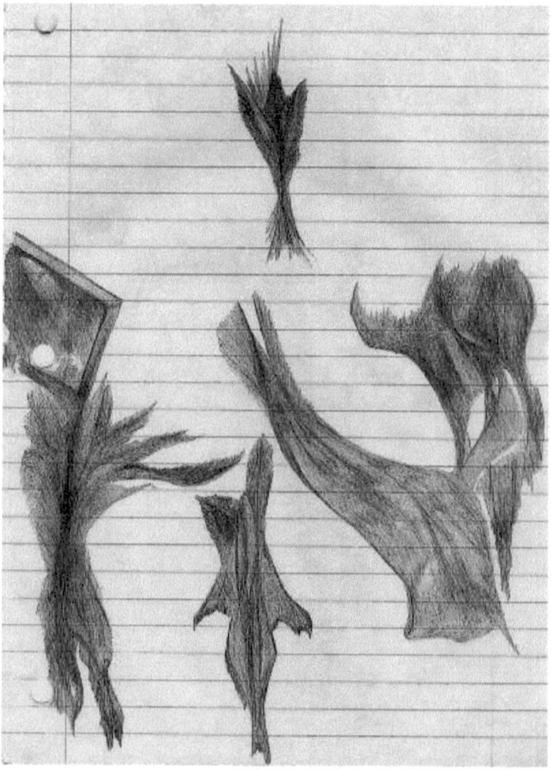

A Parrot

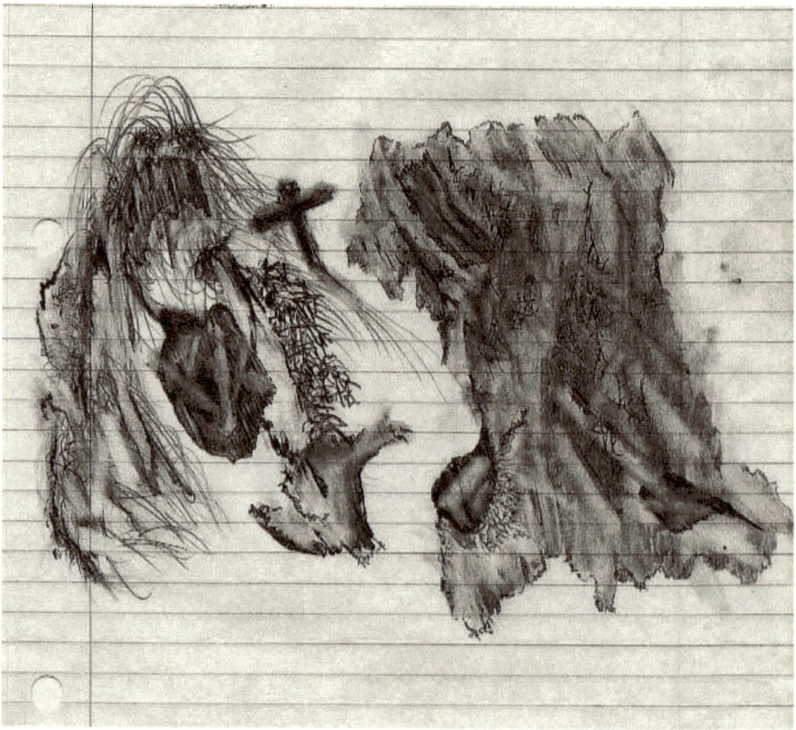

Cross and Wire

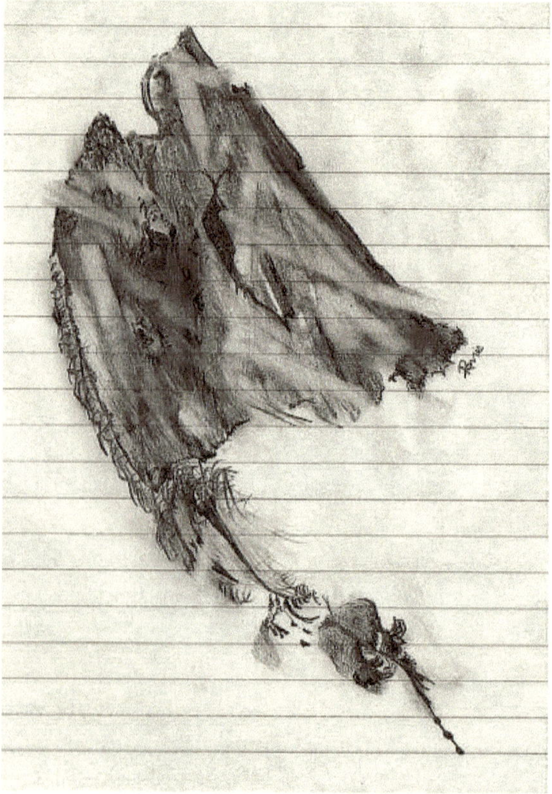

Thoughts in a Blur

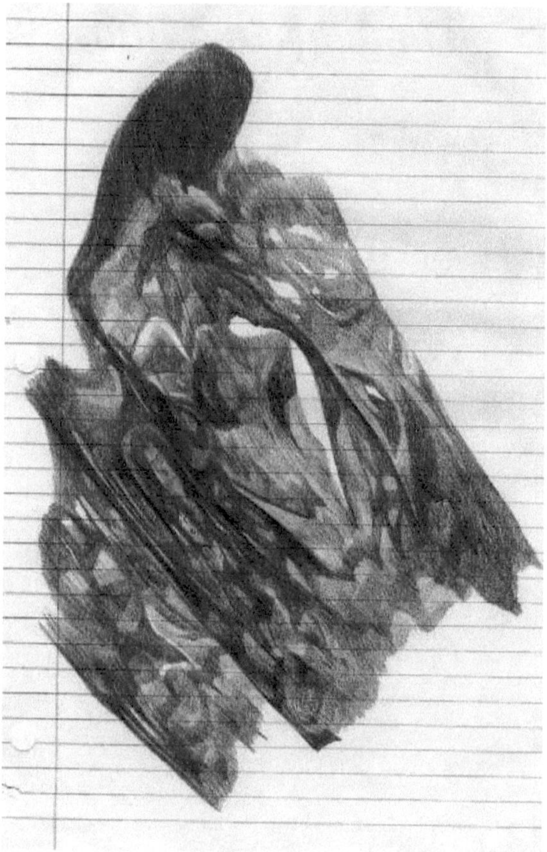

The President

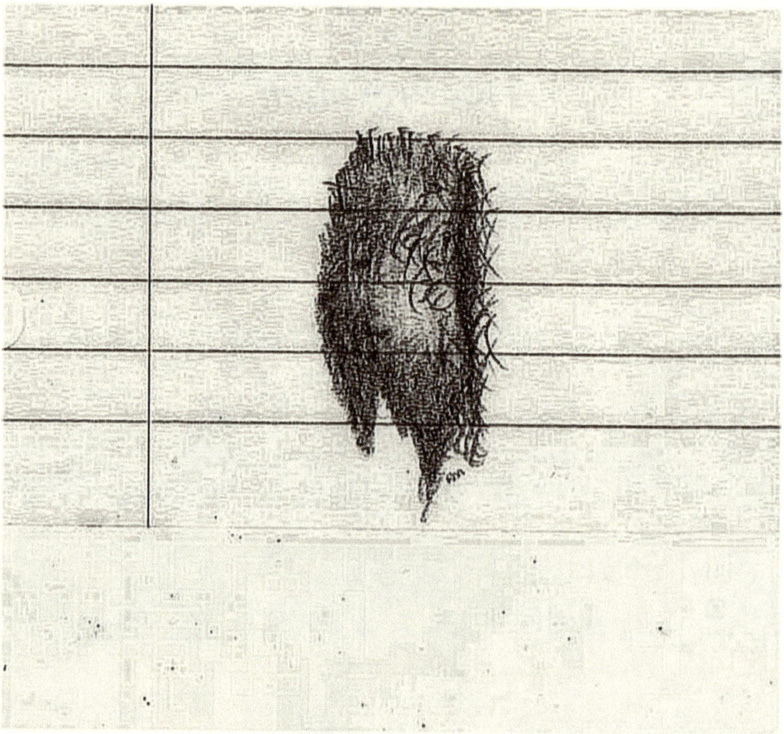

Shy

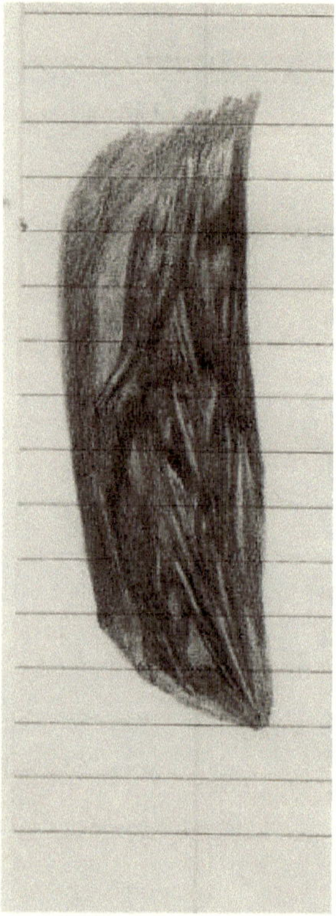

Hiding In Fear

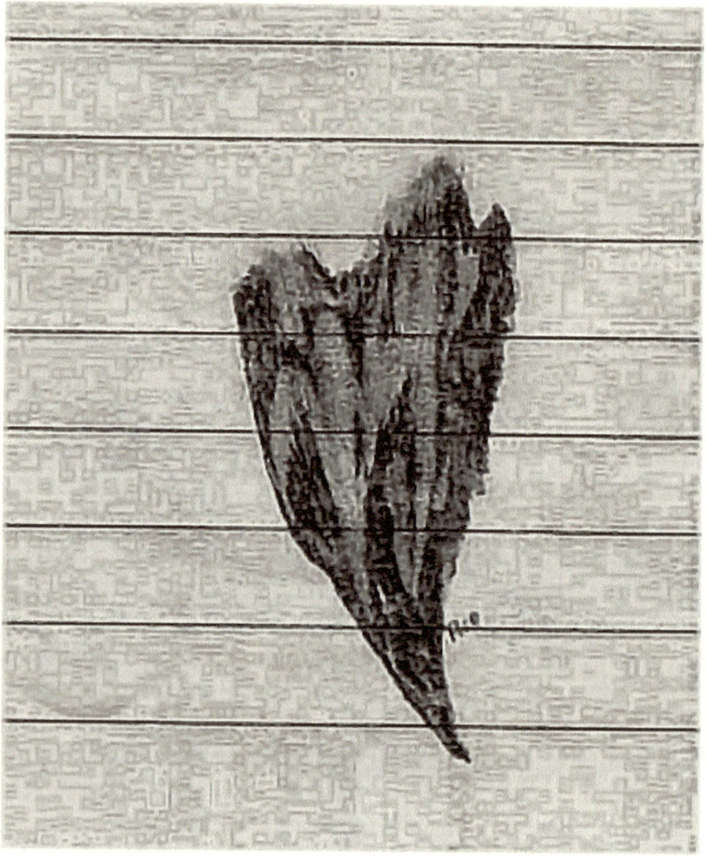

Aged Wonder

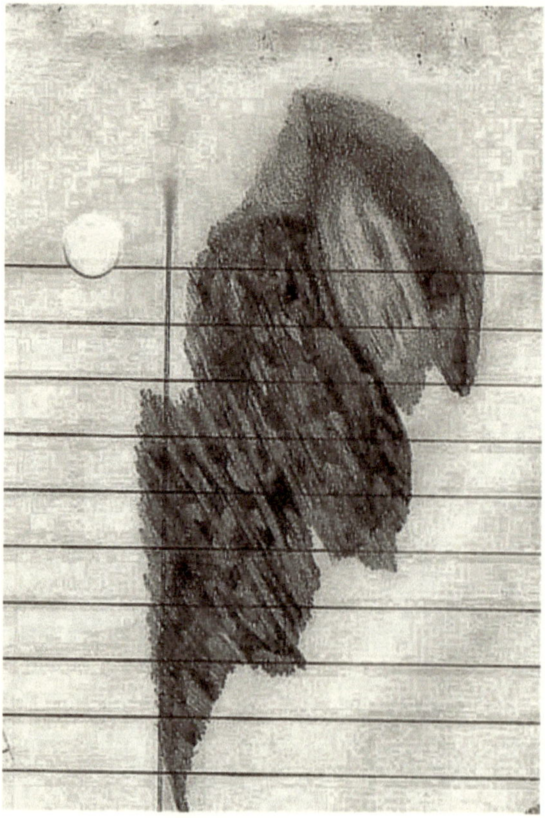

Cherub

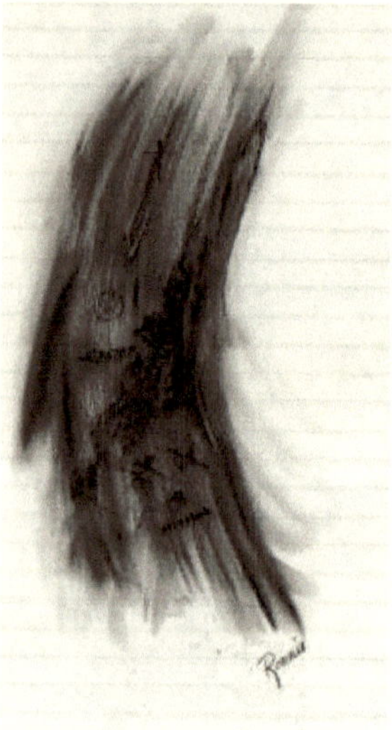

Voodoo Sleep

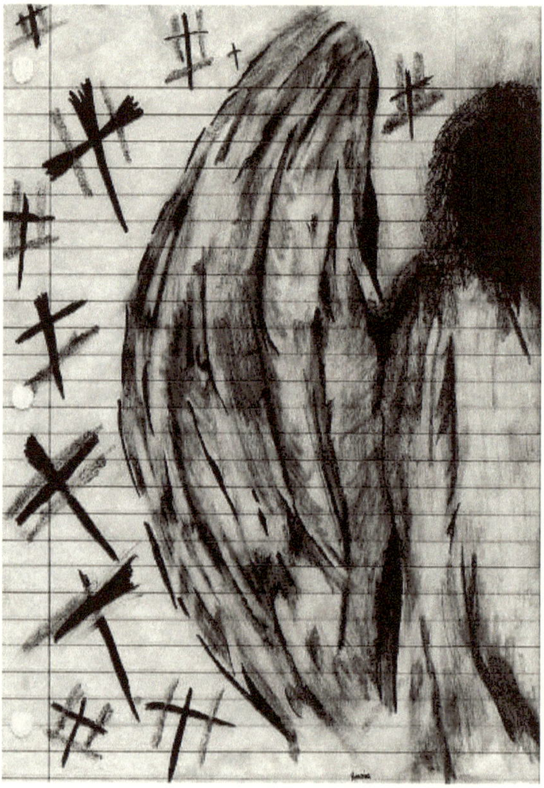

Secret Angel

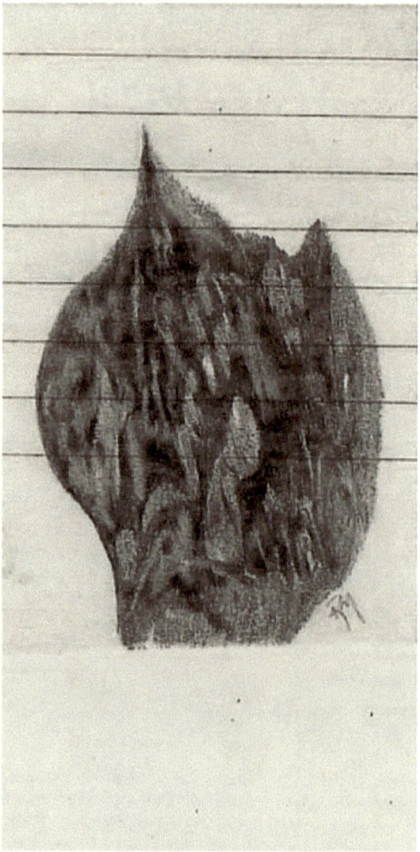

The Gathering

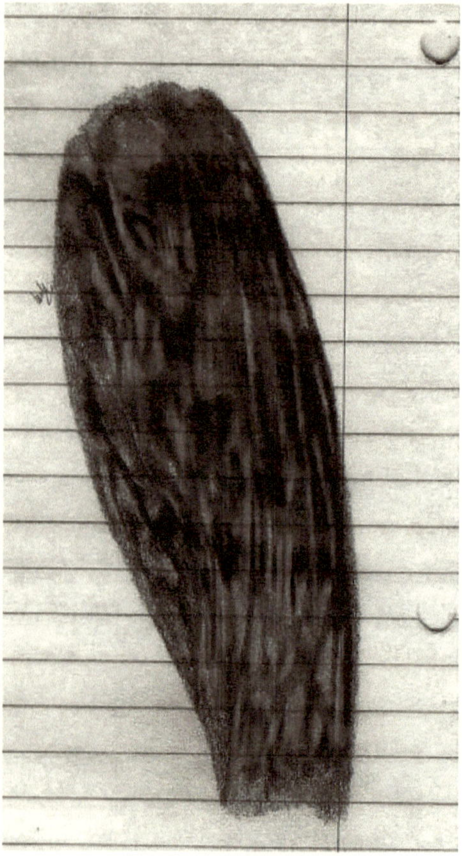

Glasses of Fire

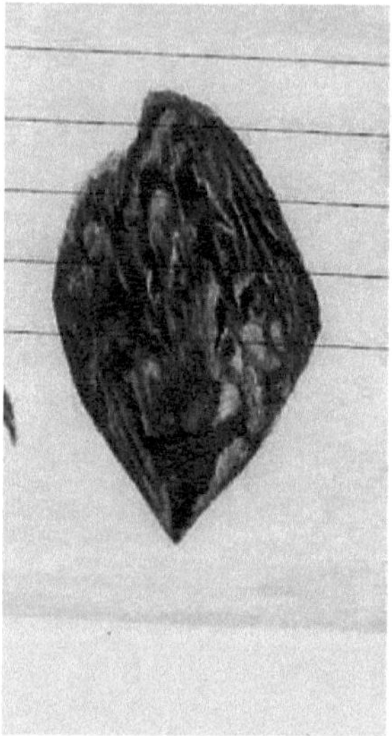

The Grin

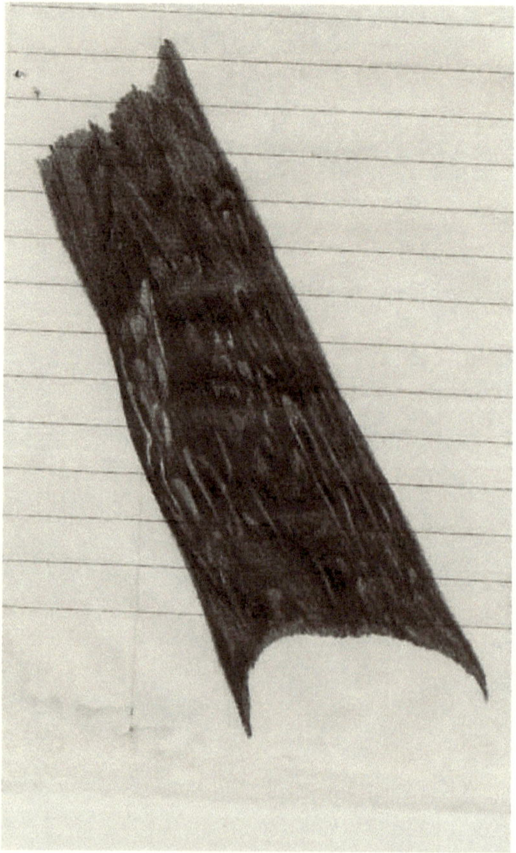

Melding Images of Fate

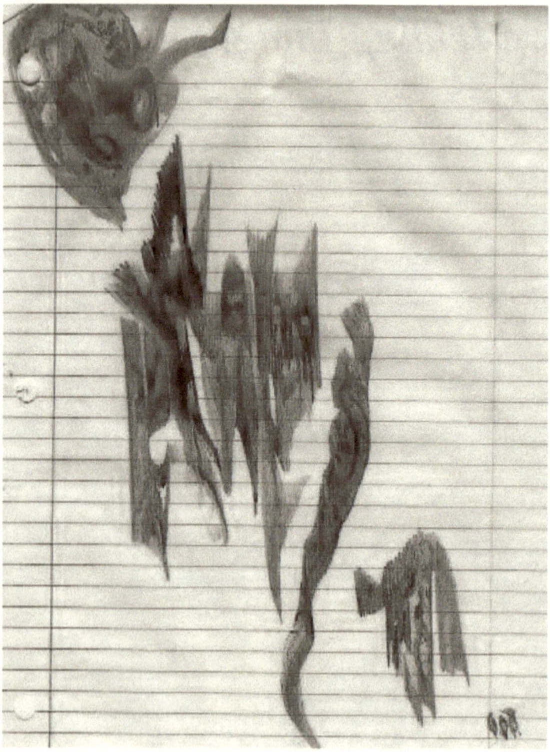

The Wolf

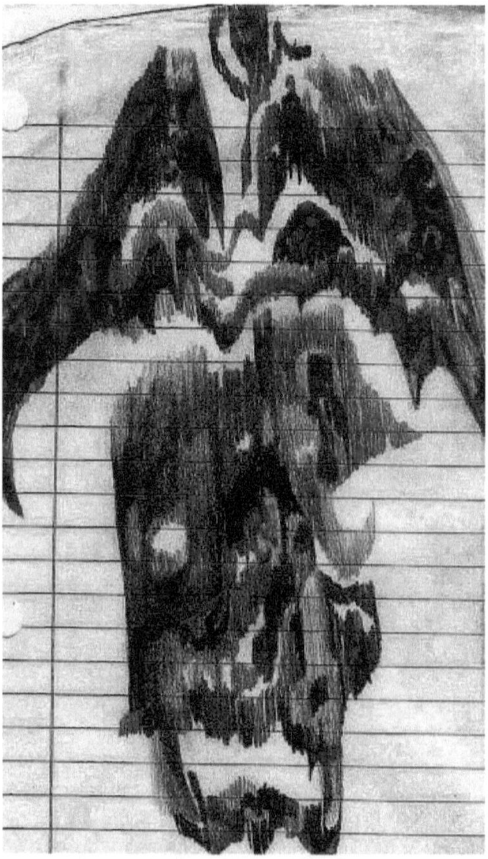

The Pirate

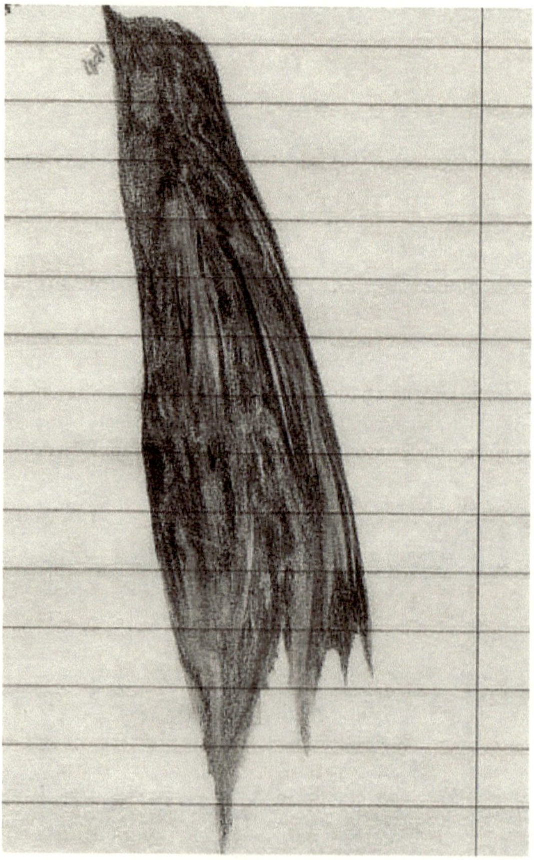

A Curtained Veil

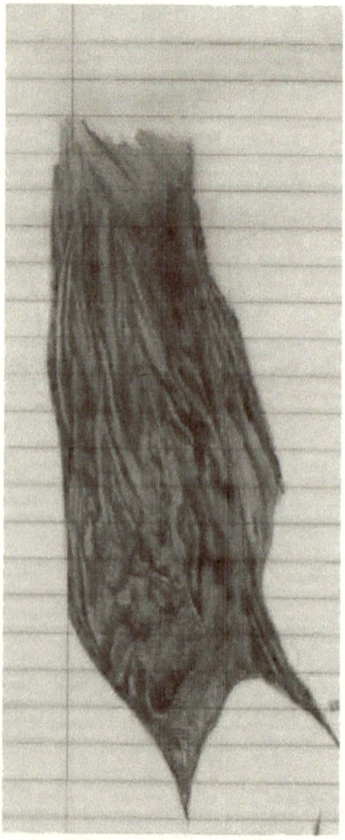

The Devils Veil

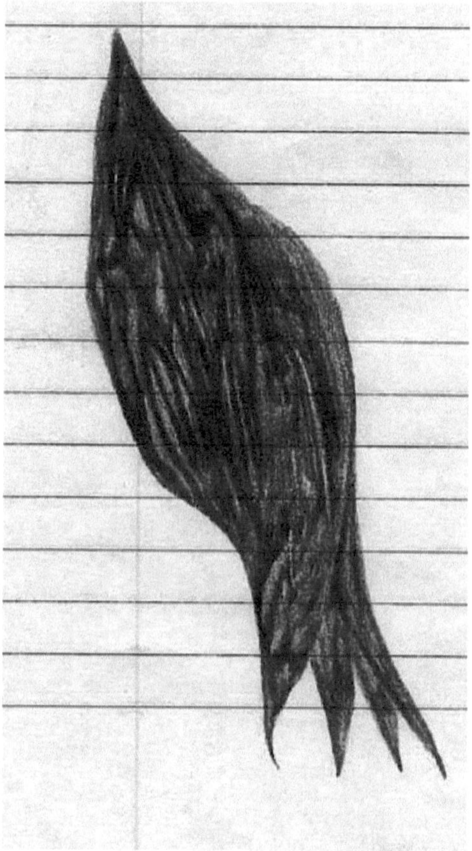

A Greeting

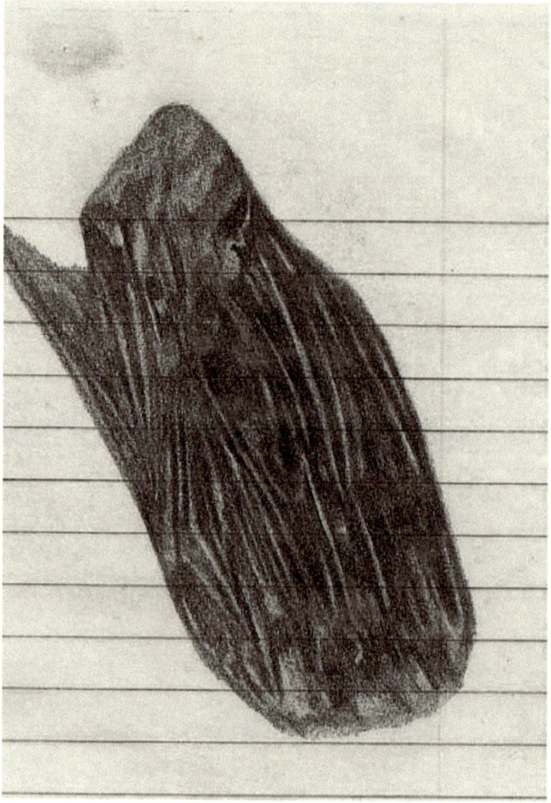

Lost In The Woods

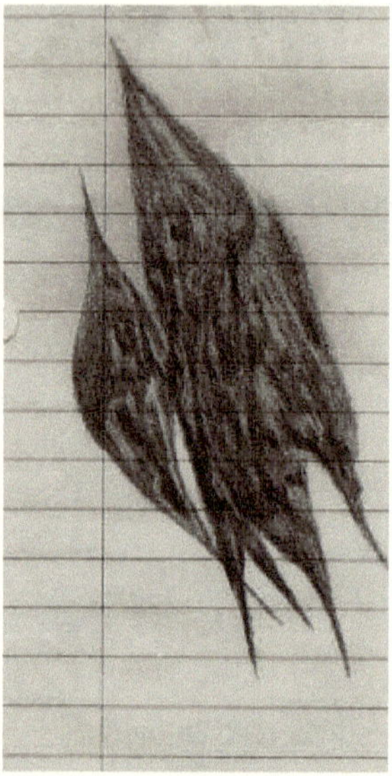

The Gnome

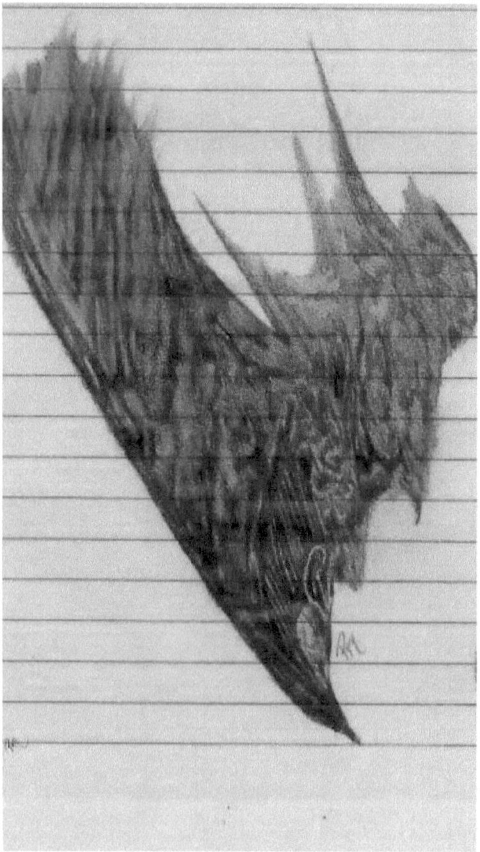

Sled to Eternity

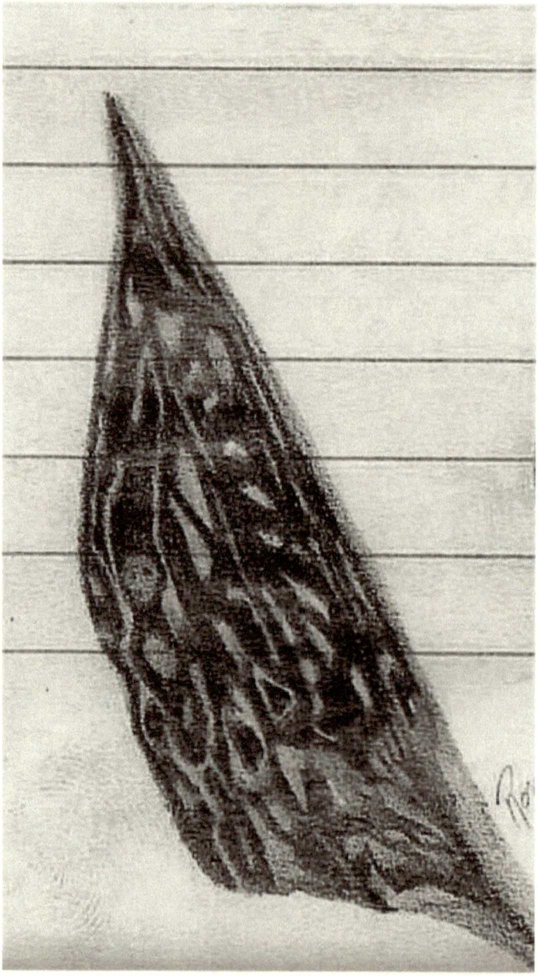

Lost In The Wilderness

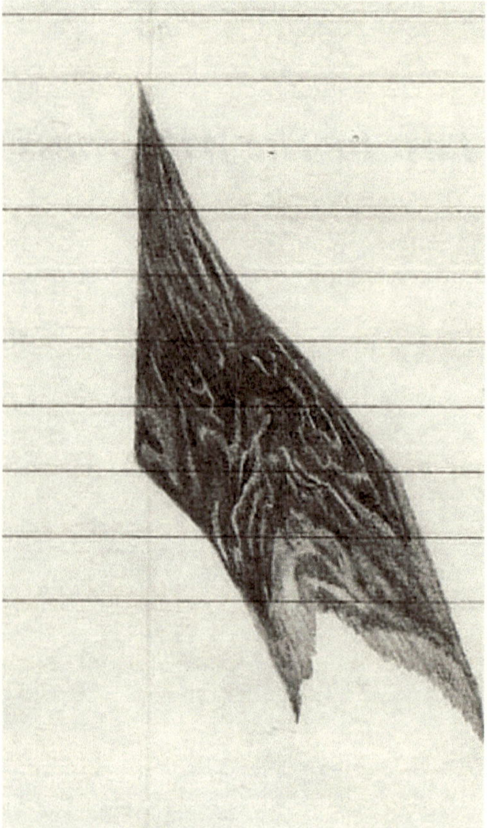

Shadows

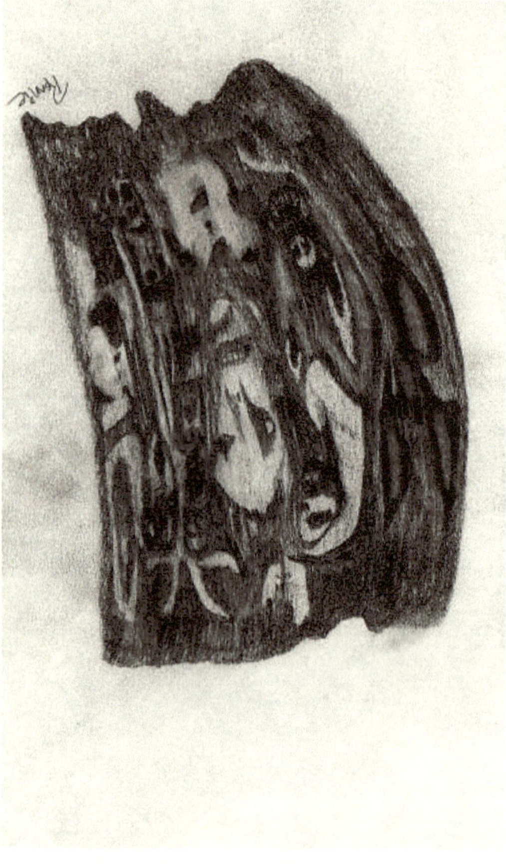

Muscles

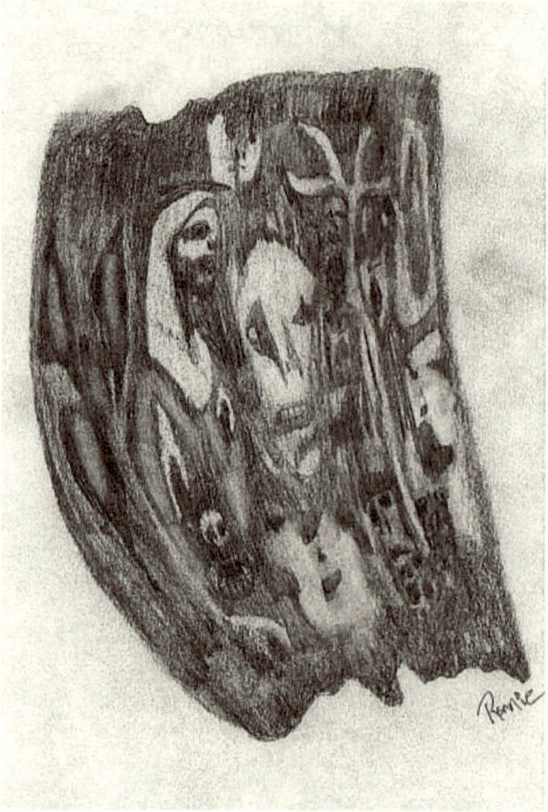

Strong

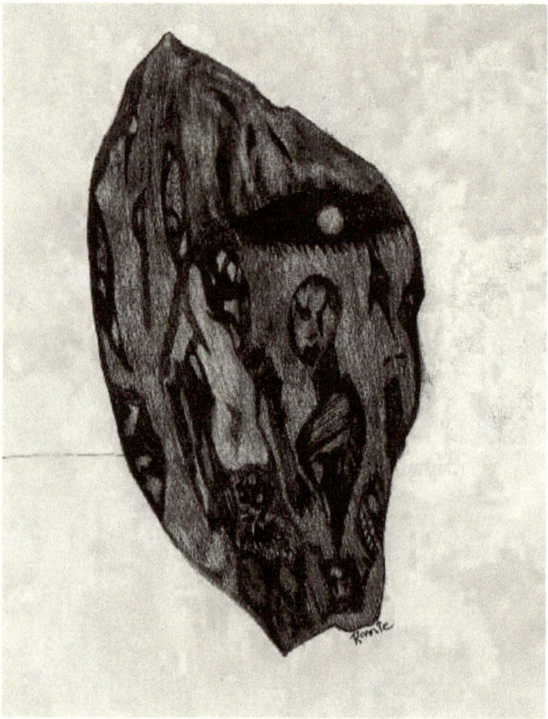

The Eye

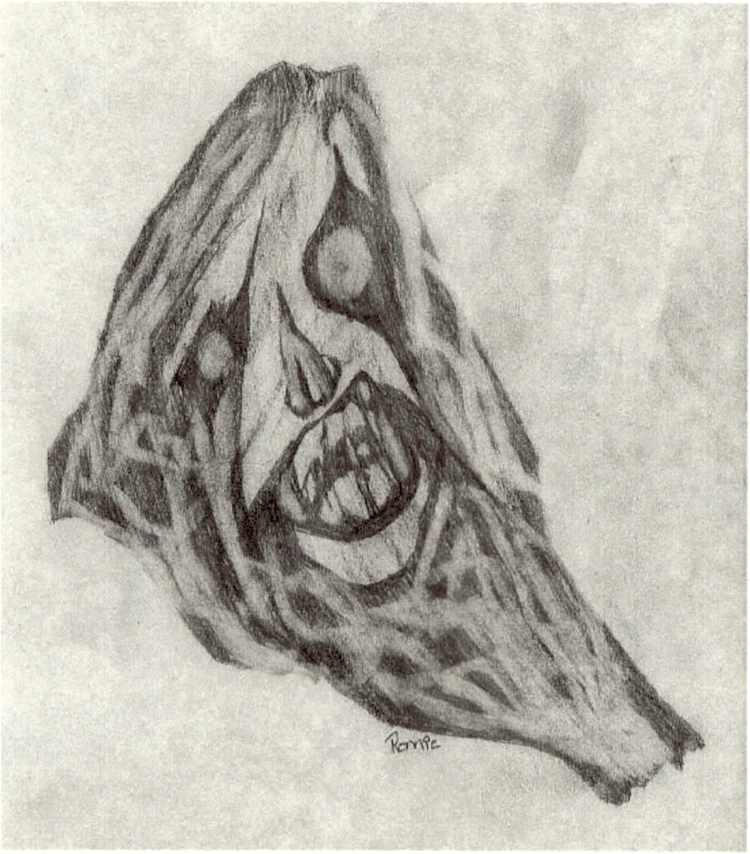

Zombie Eyed

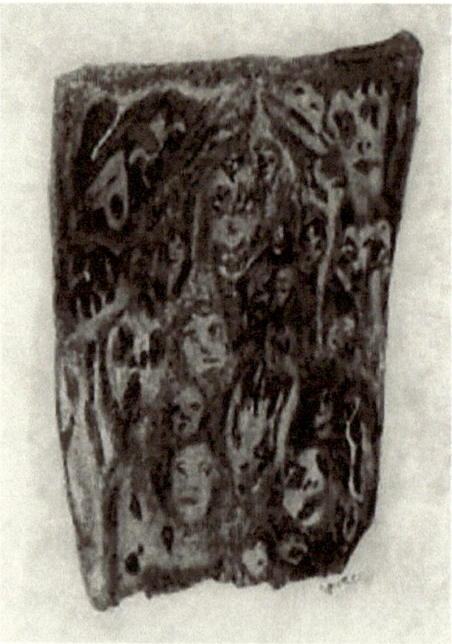

Fresh Dreams And Nightmares

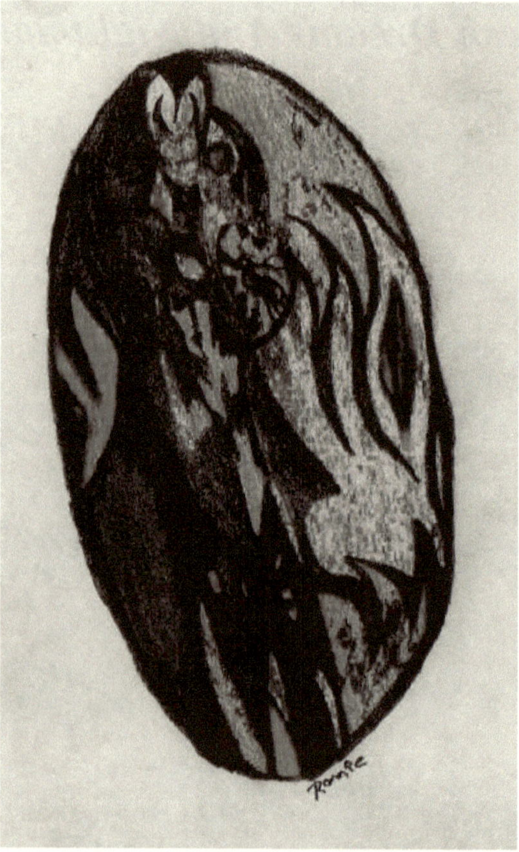

Lady Hawk

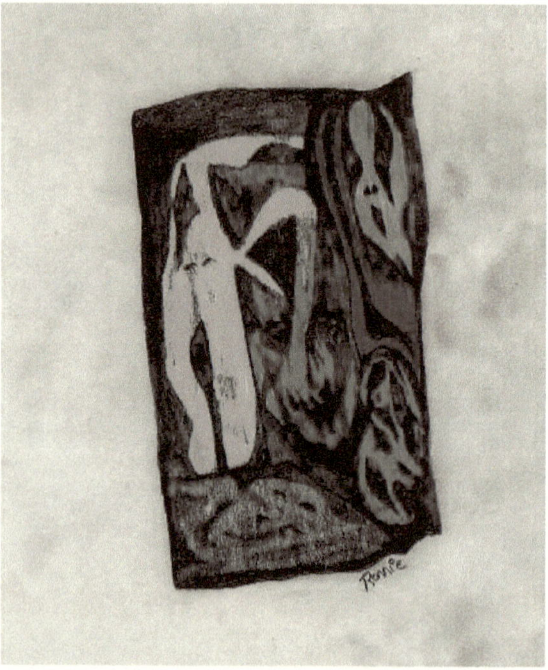
Ronnie

Portrait

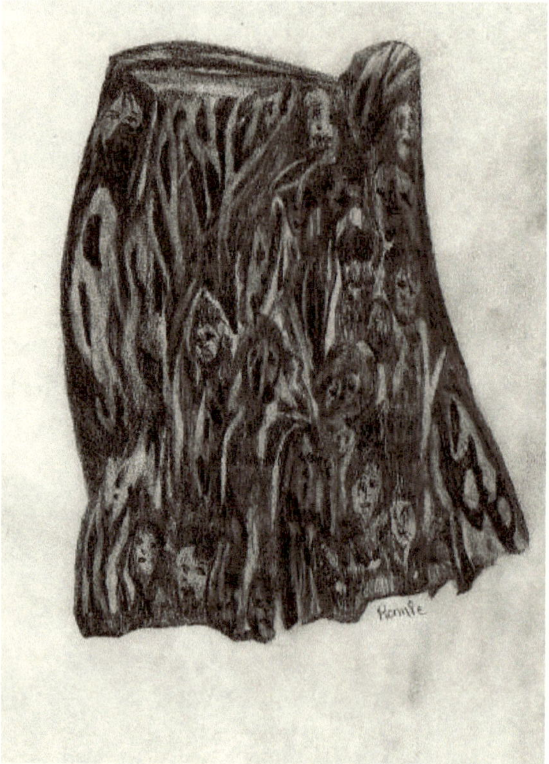
Ronnie

The Gaurds Vision

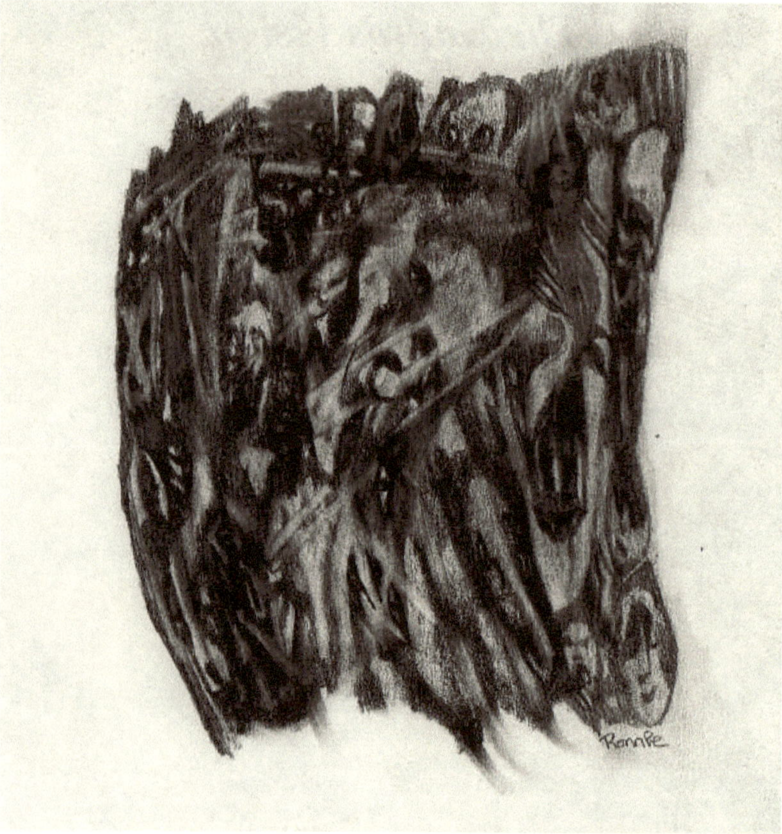

Dreams of Gray Rain

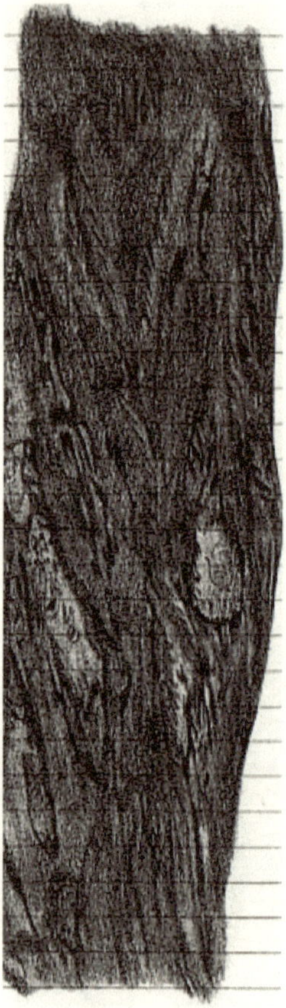

Flames

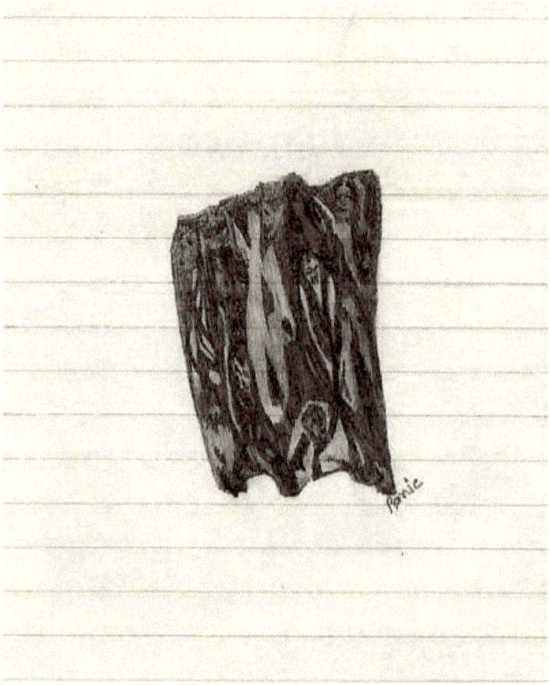

Standing In Shadow

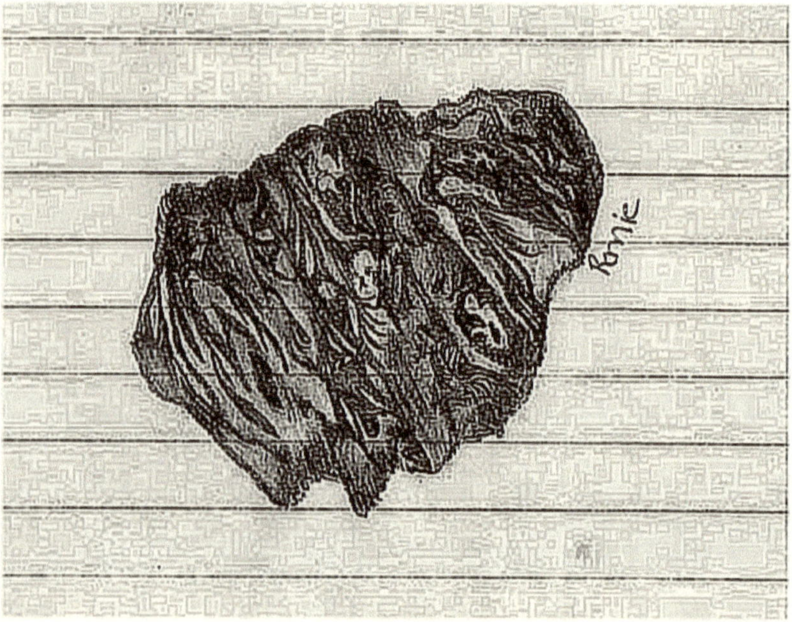
Ronnie

Everything In A Dream

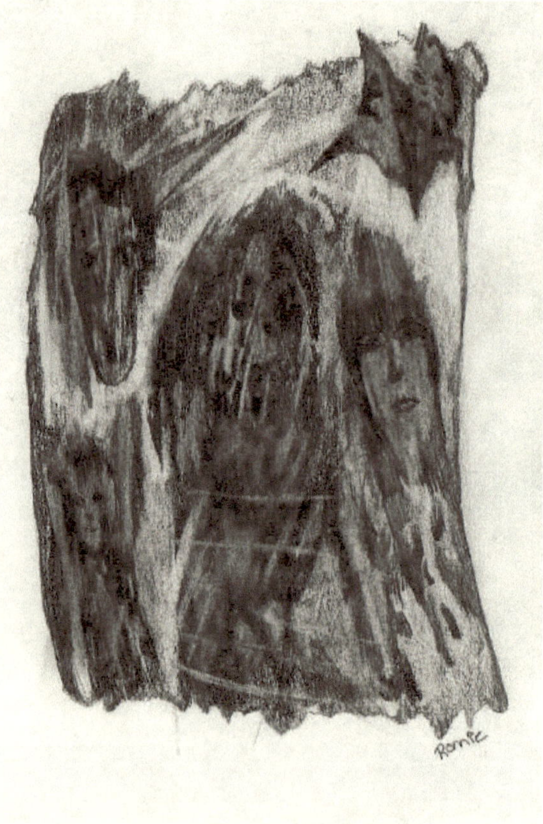
Ronie

Her Crazy Thought

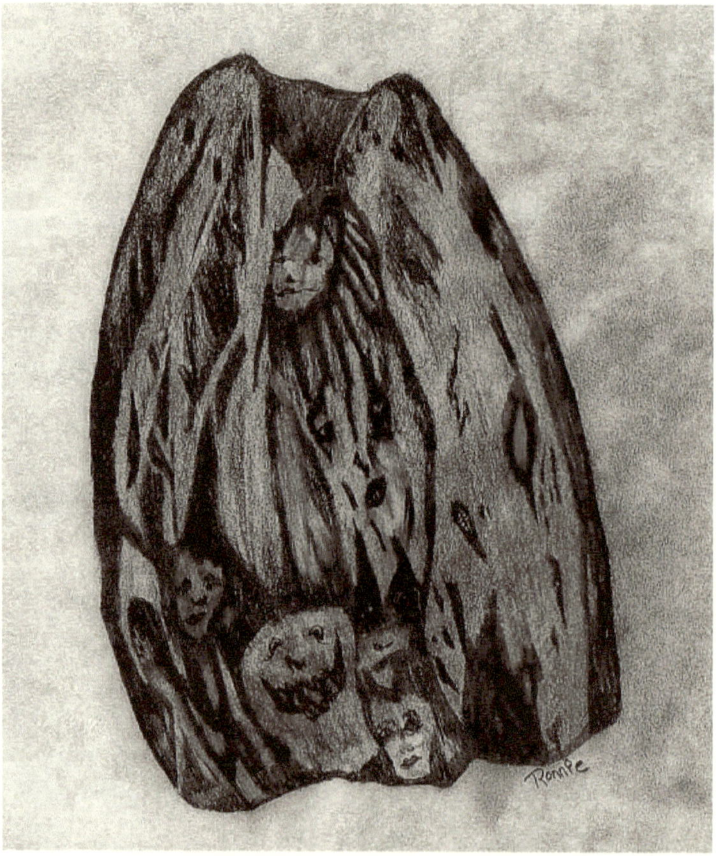
Ronnie

Sun Goddess

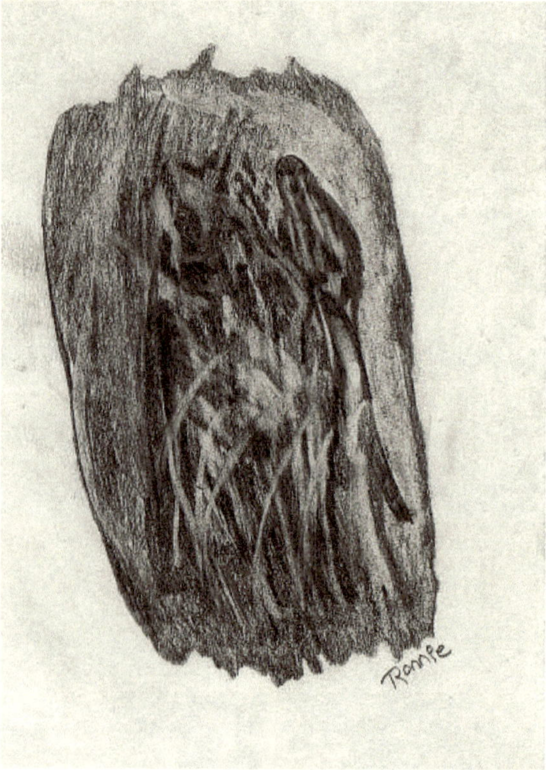
Ronnie

The Woman And The Crow

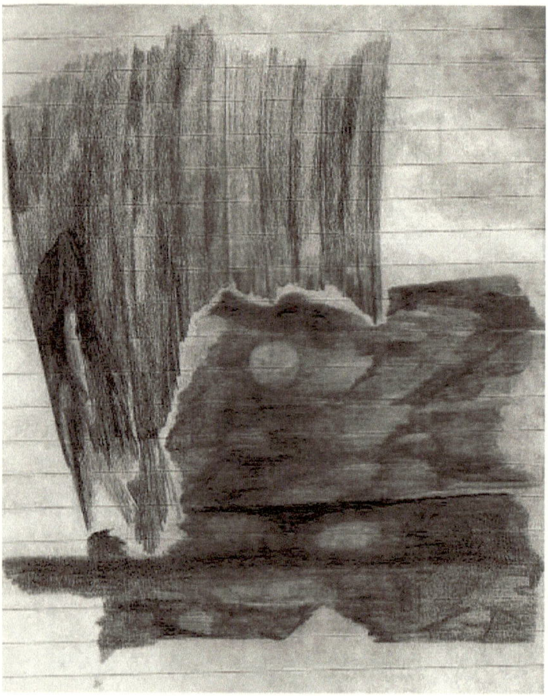

The Moons Reflection

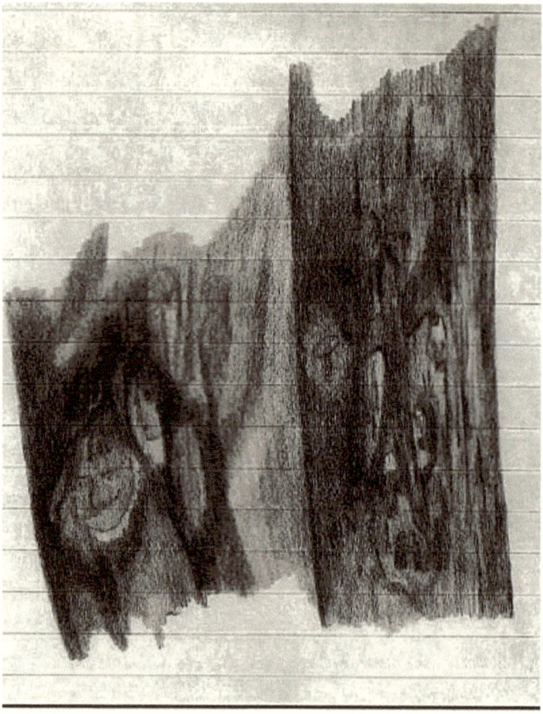

Regal Reflections

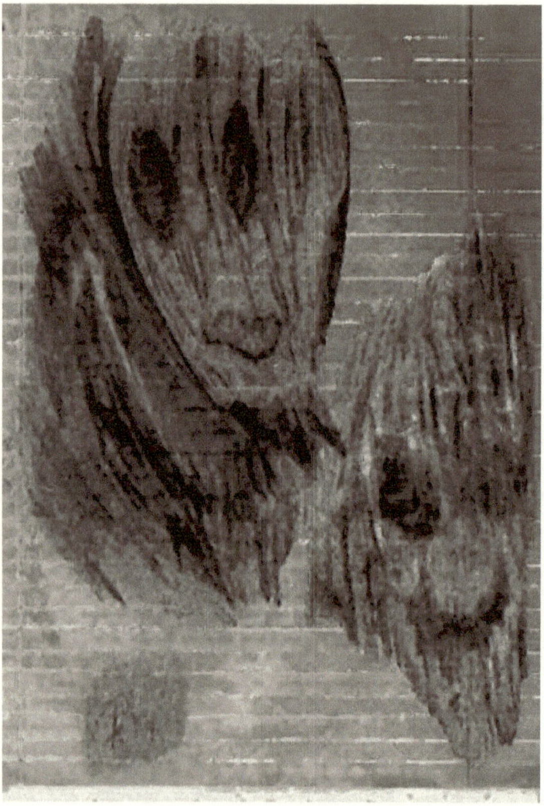

Hidden Secrets of Appearance

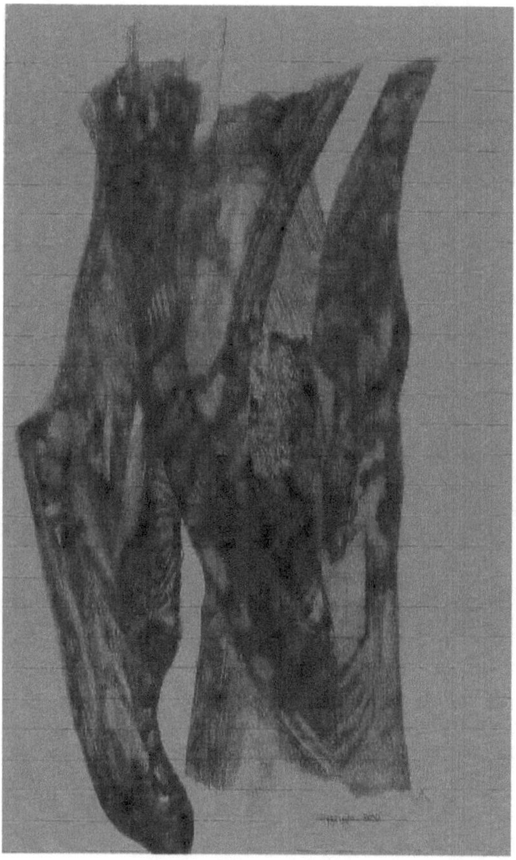

Butterfly In Red

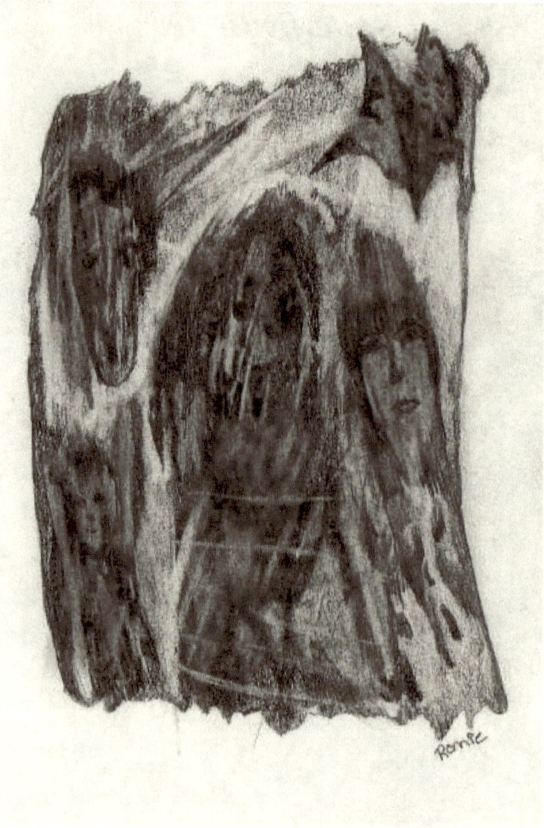
Ronie

Her Crazy Thought

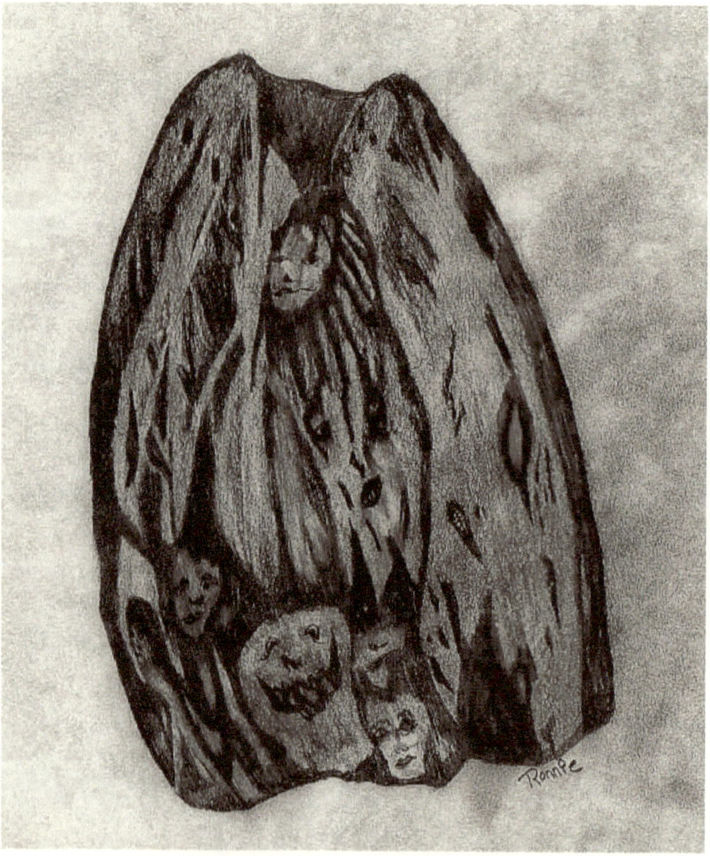

Sun Goddess

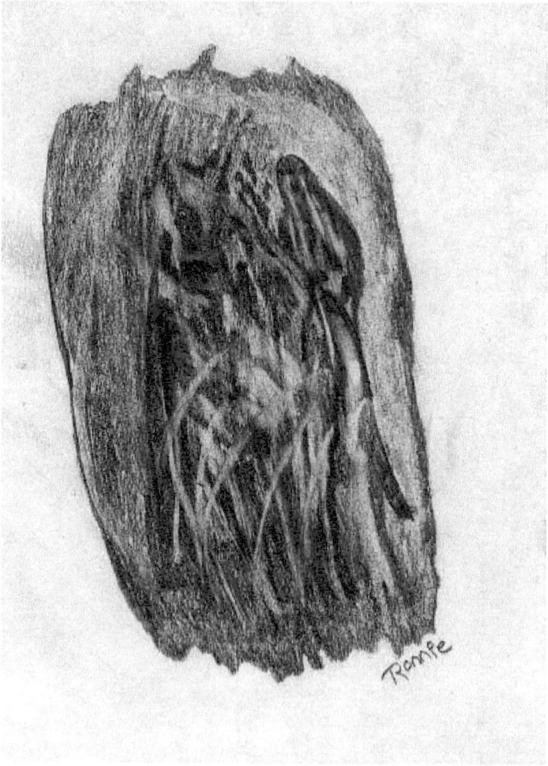
Ronnie

The Woman and the Crow

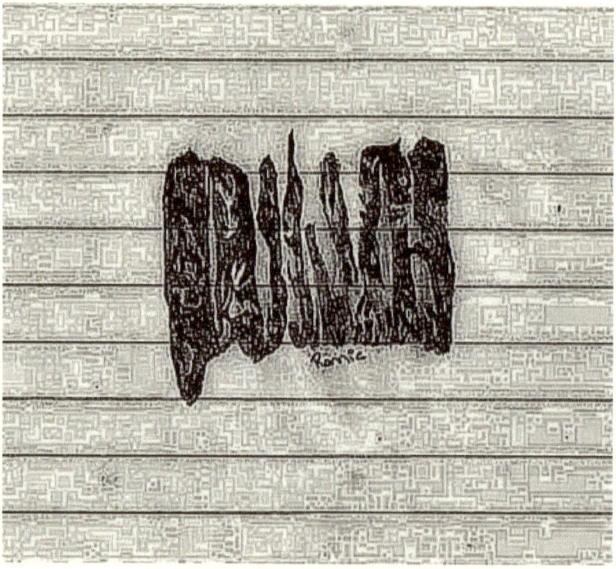

Small Images

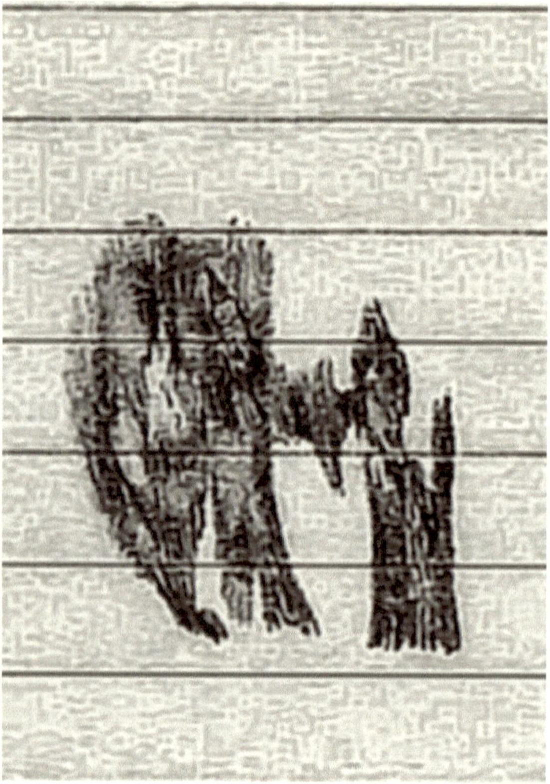

Royal Parade

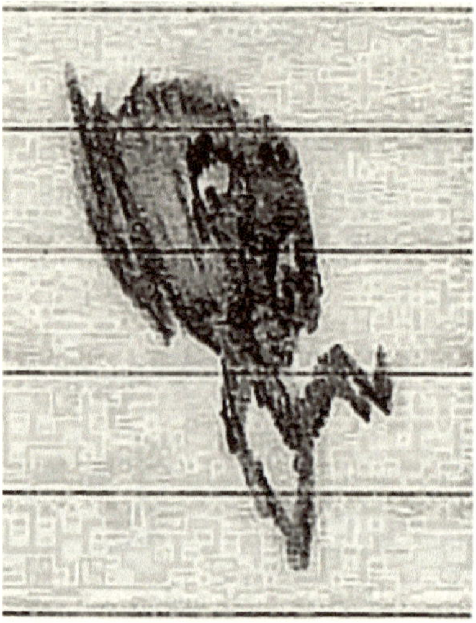

The Swing

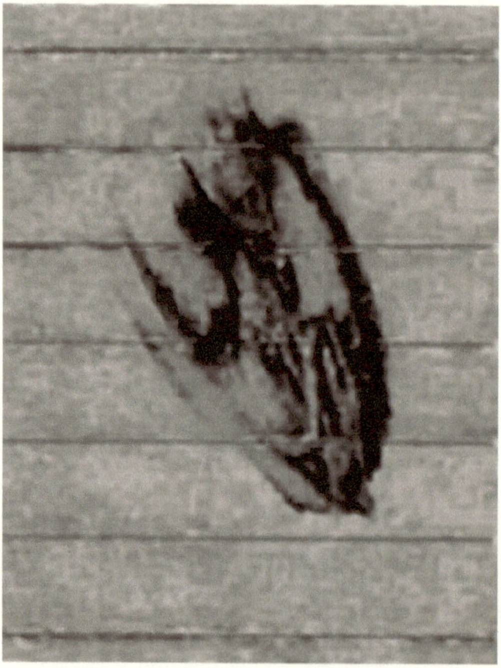

The Blurry Season

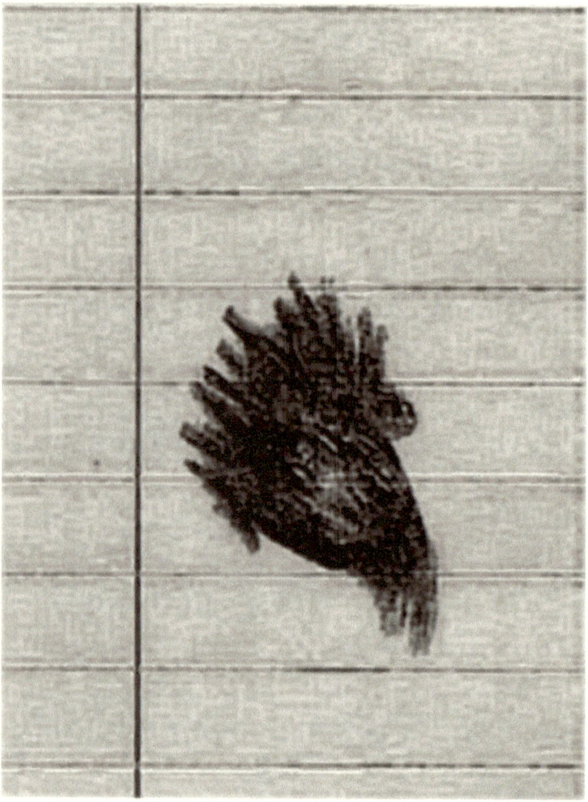

The Wanderer

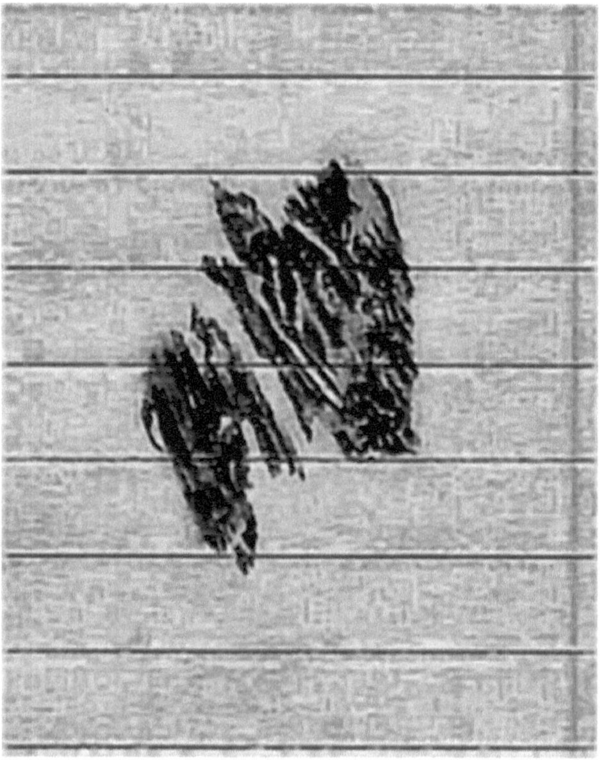

Jumbled Mirage

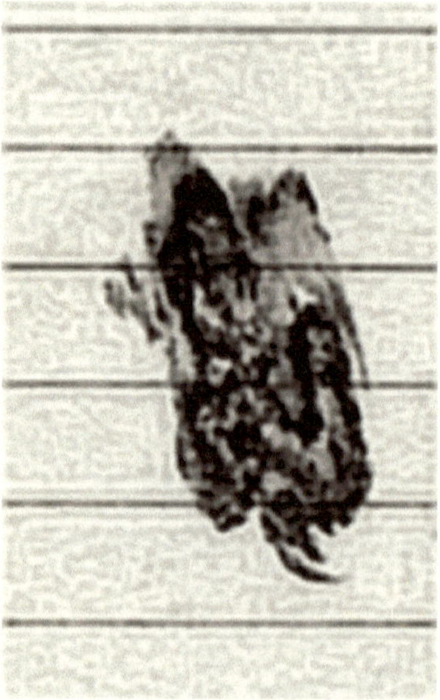

Man In Mystery

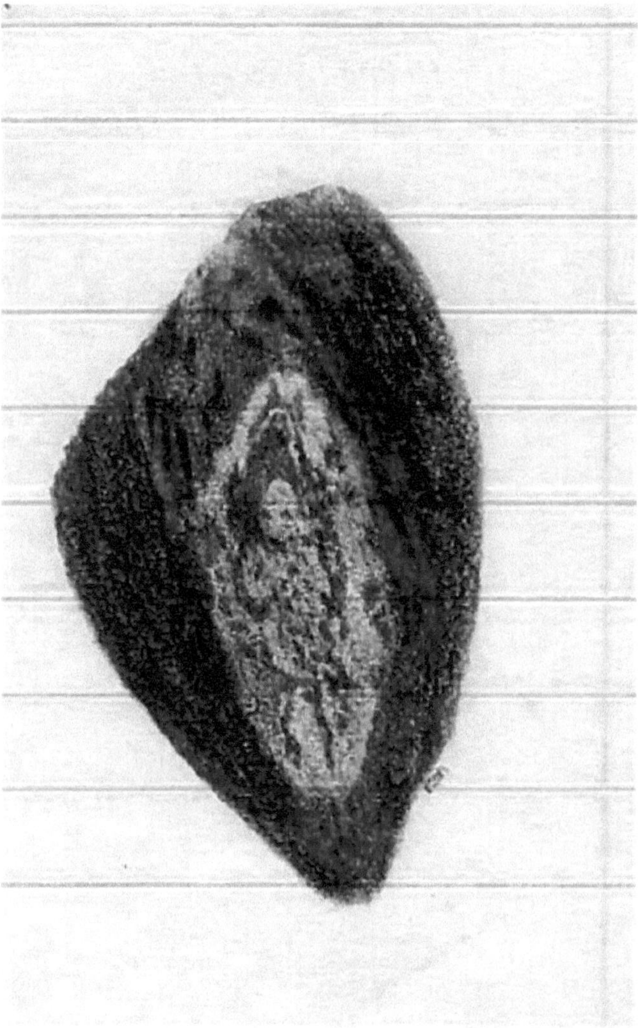

Hiding In Secret

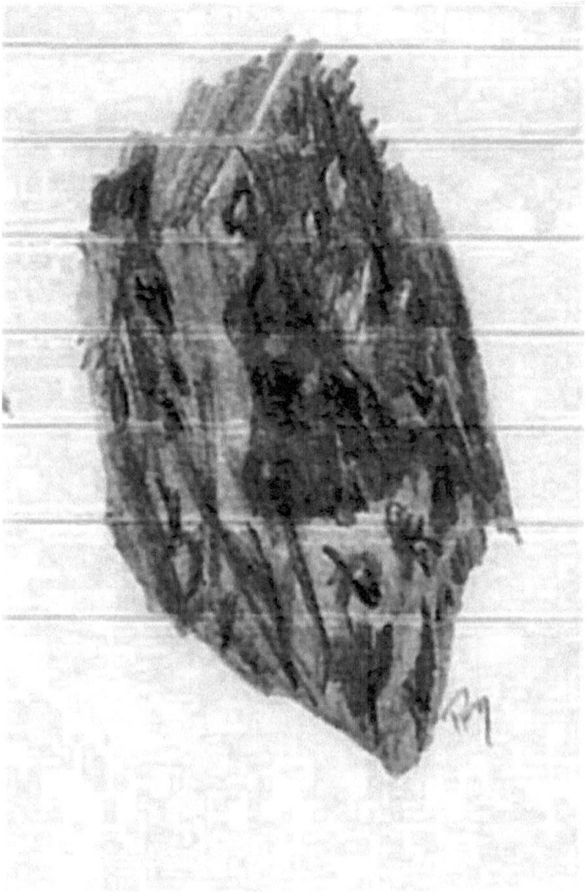

Royal Walk

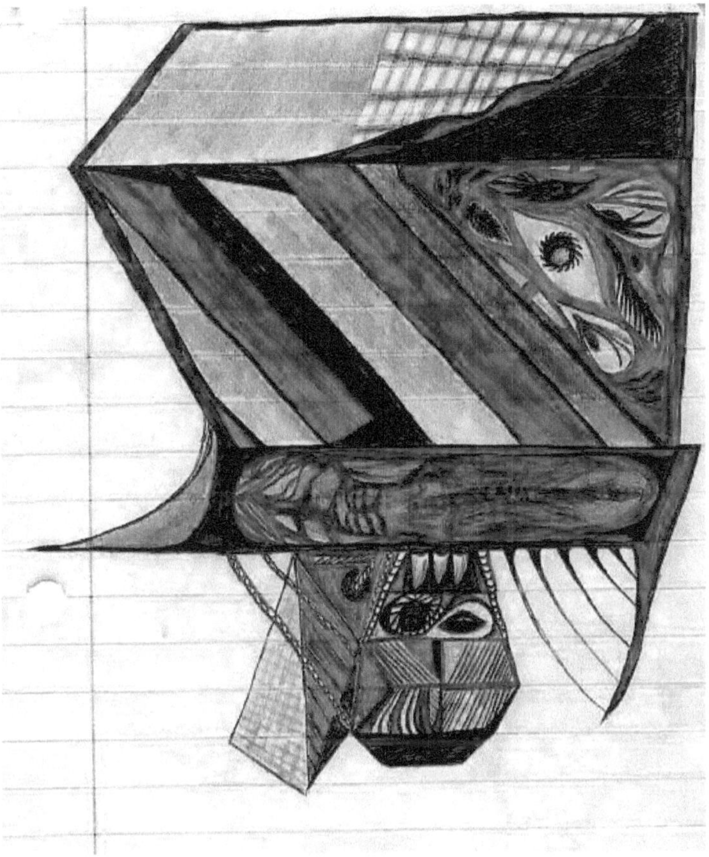

Mirrors

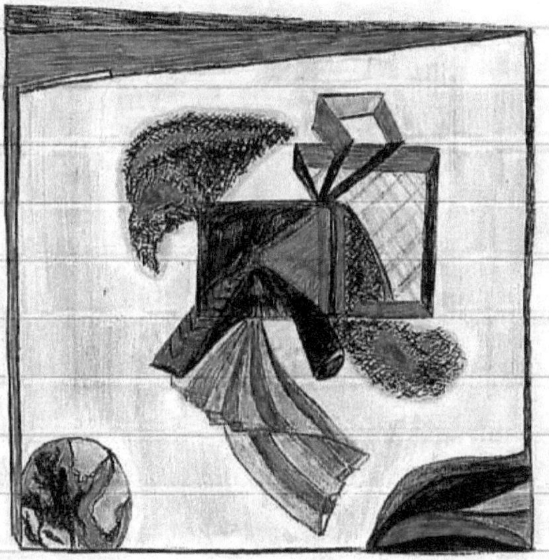

The Cube

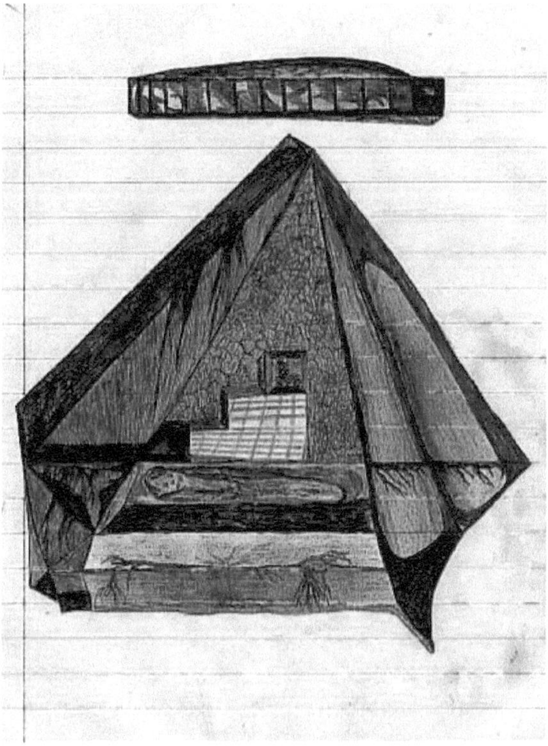

The Burial

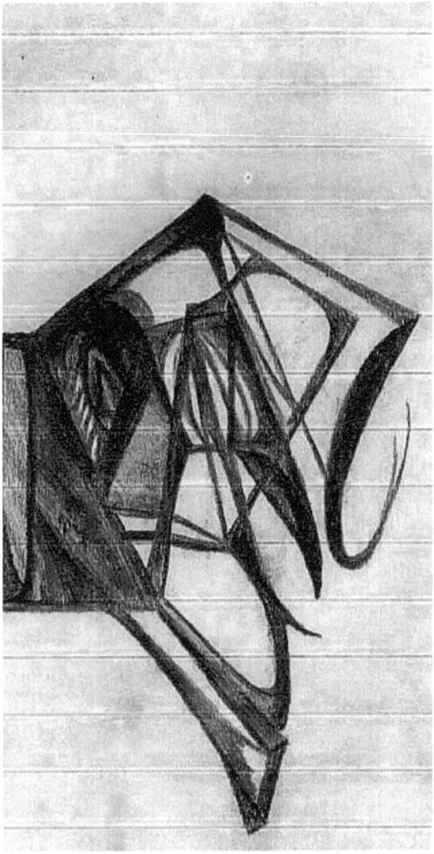

Angles Unfolding

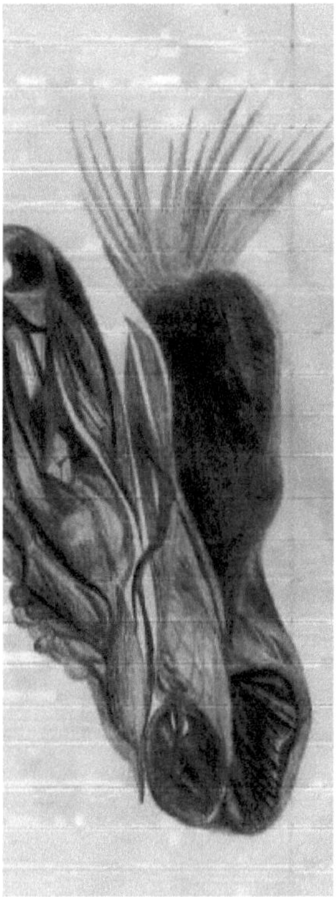

A Tuft of Crabgrass

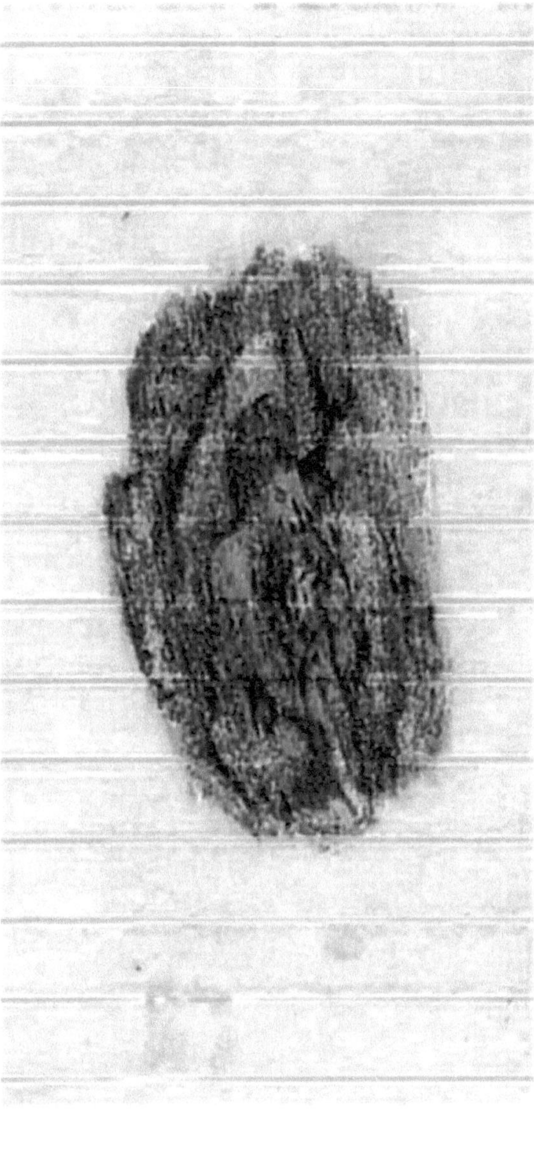

Mother and Daughter

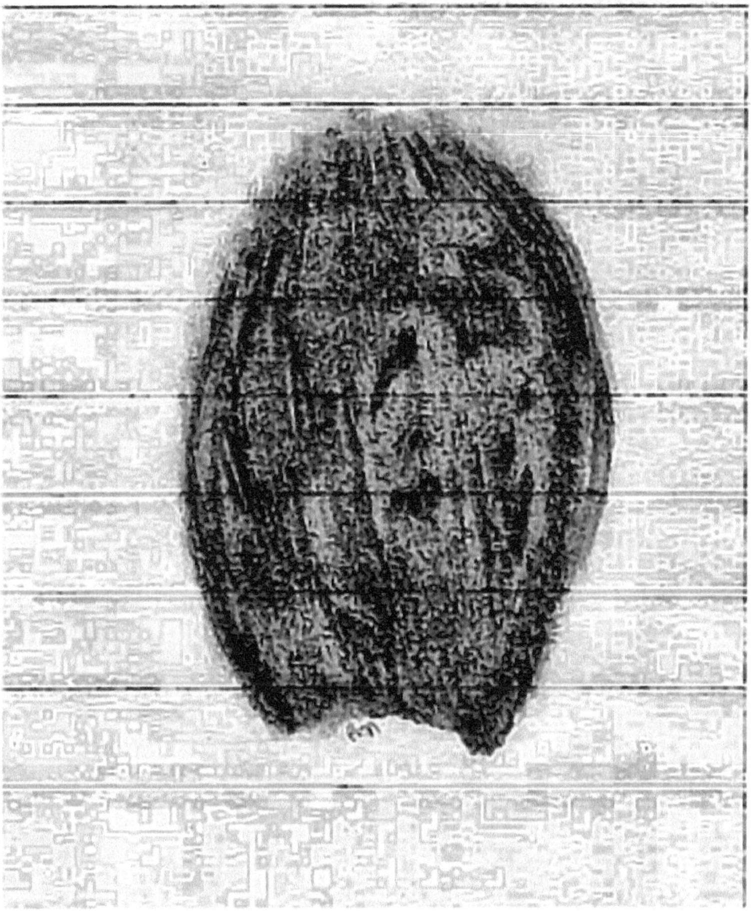

Horns

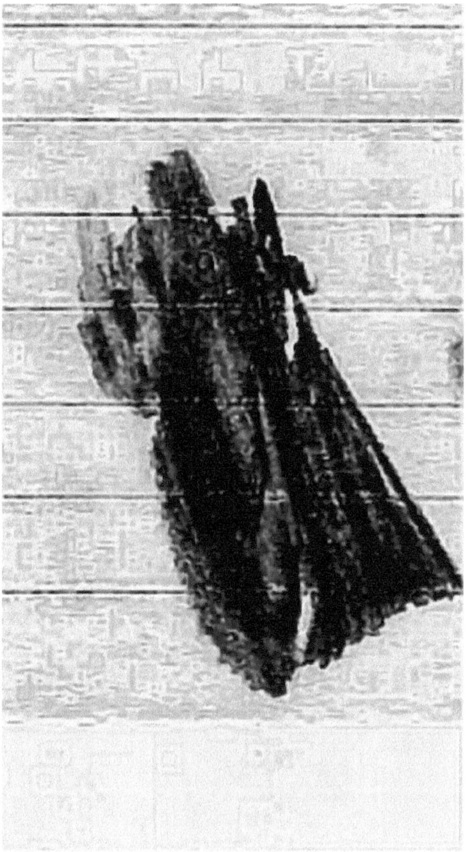

Standing Tall

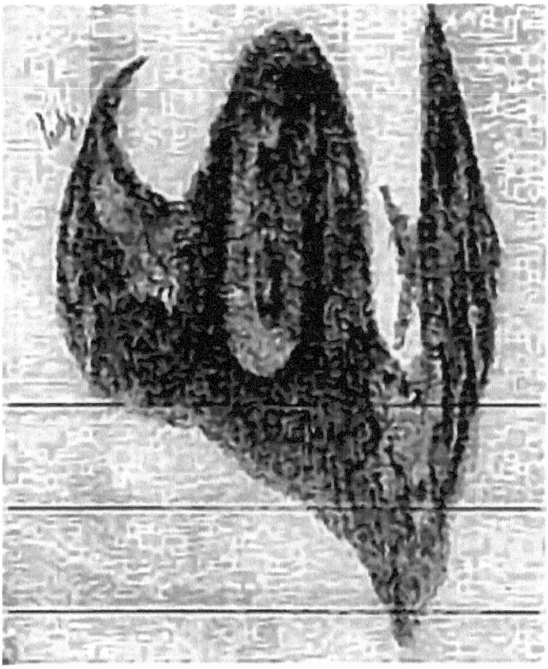

Images of Faith

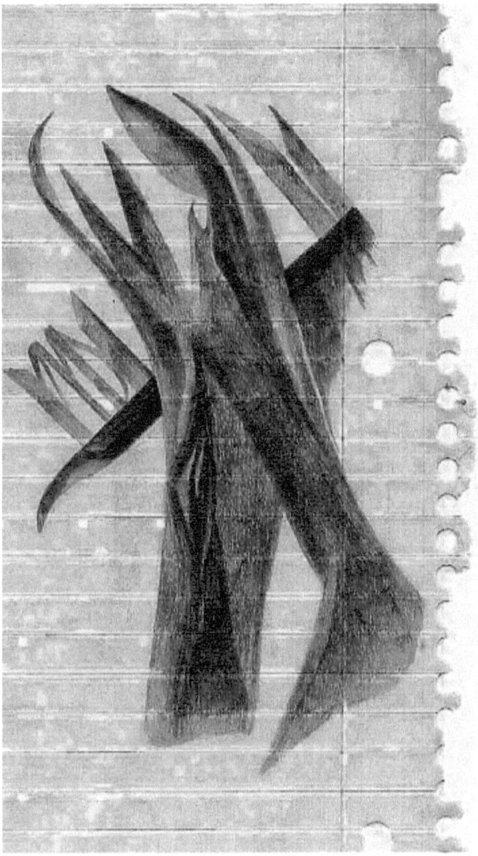

Images in Gray

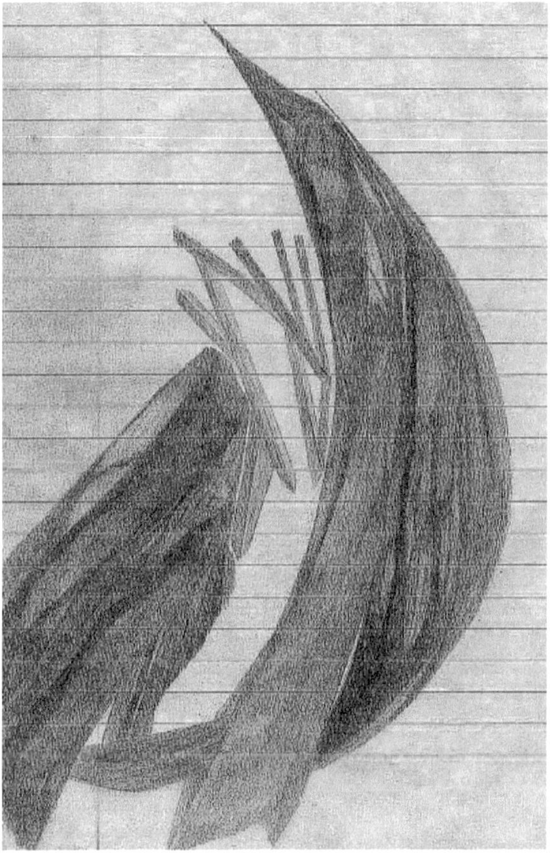

Cresent Moon

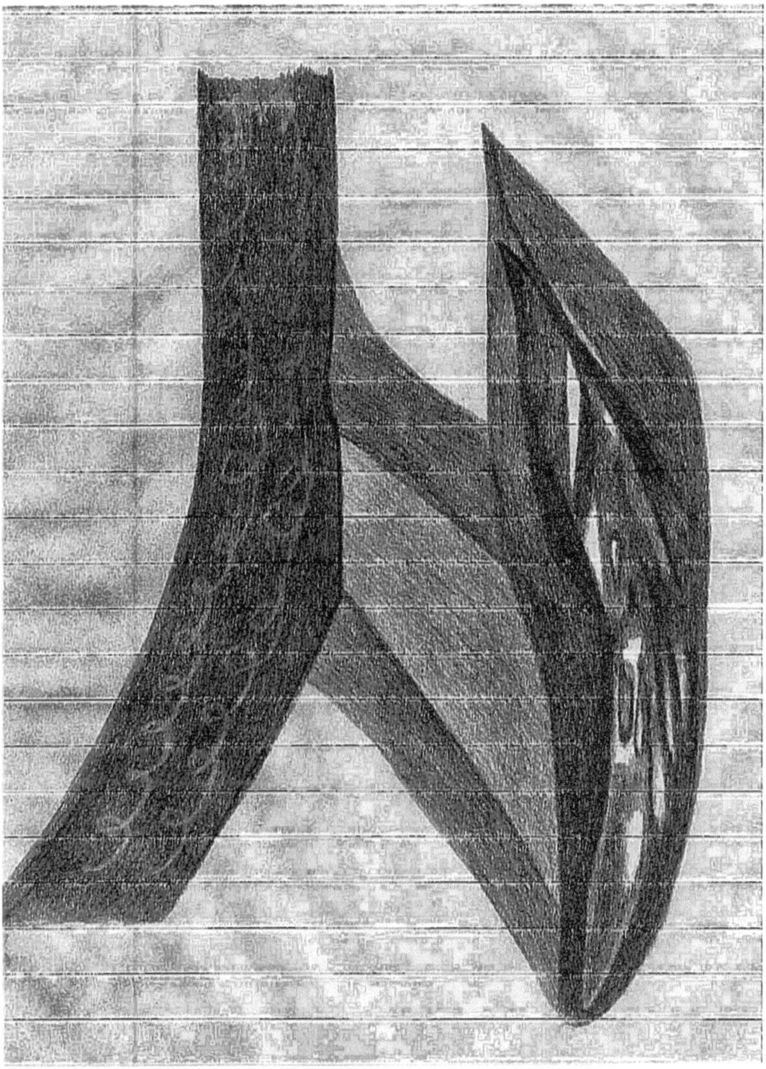

Fear In Steps

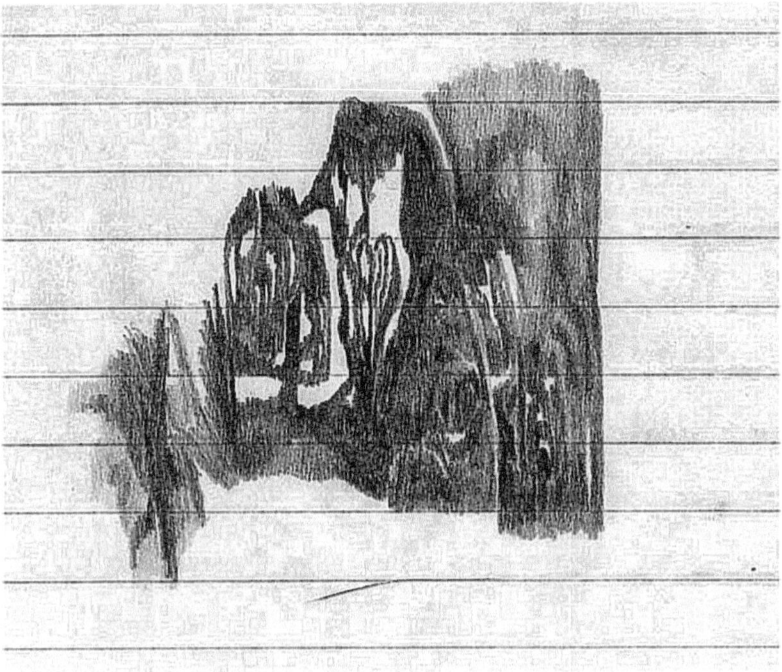

A Reflection Of Sanity

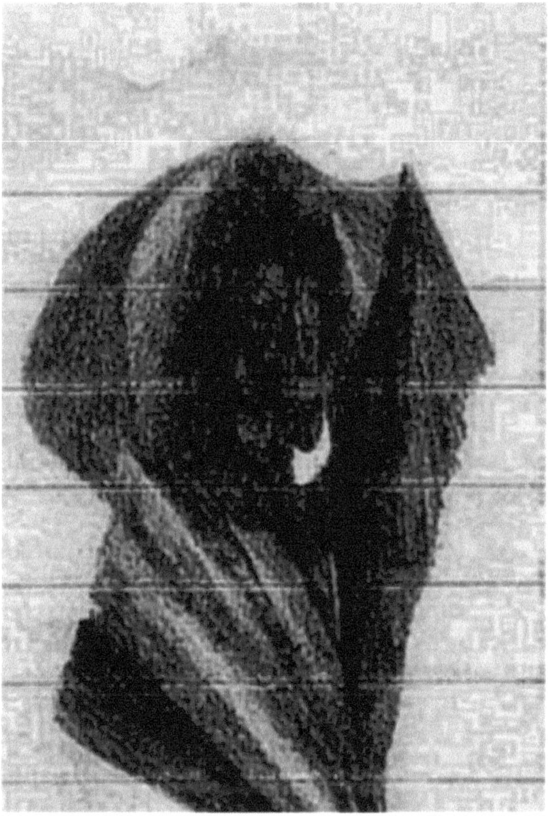

Arrayed

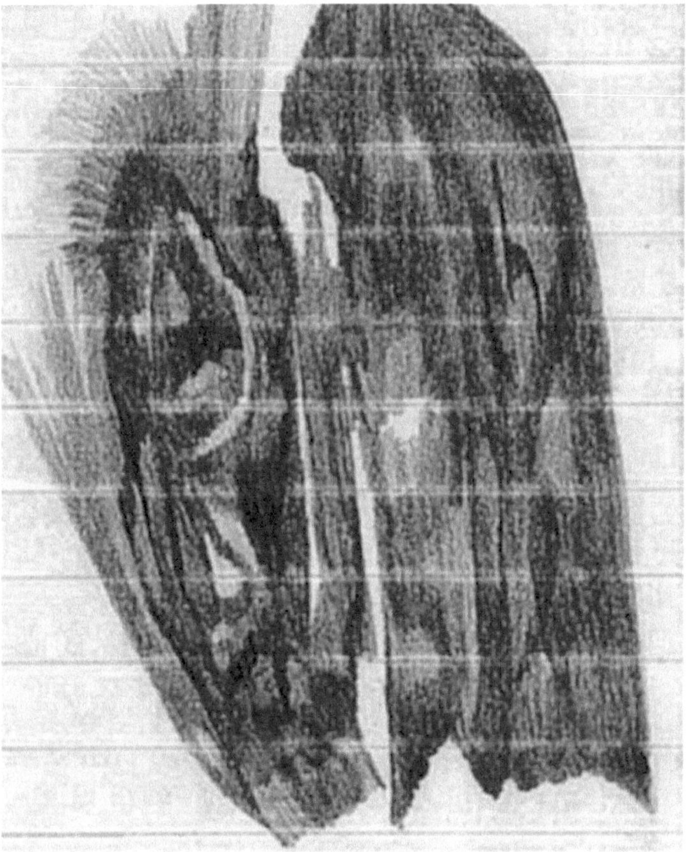

Monsters Among Us

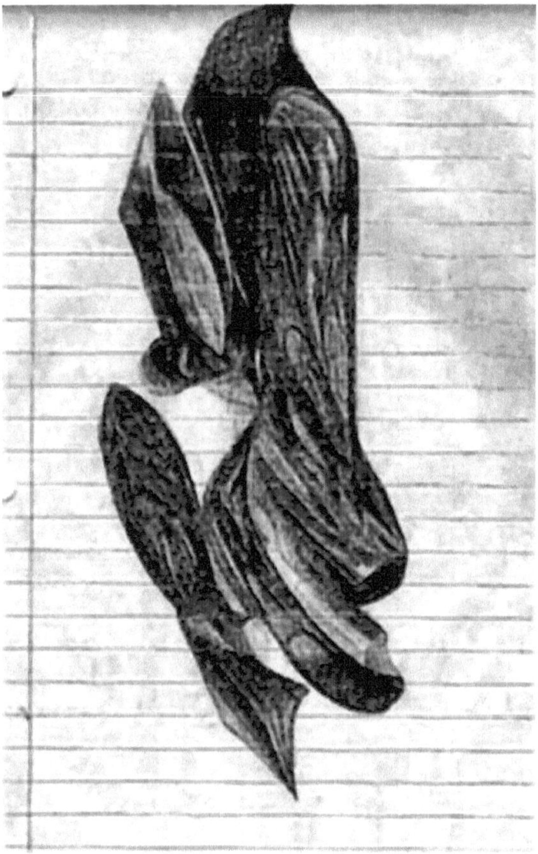

Vivid Slices

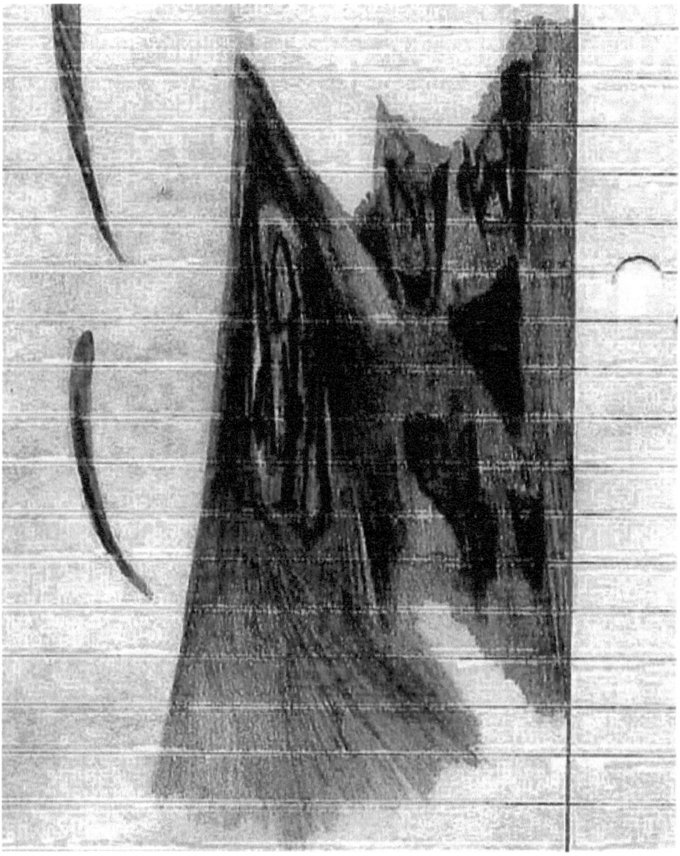

The Windows

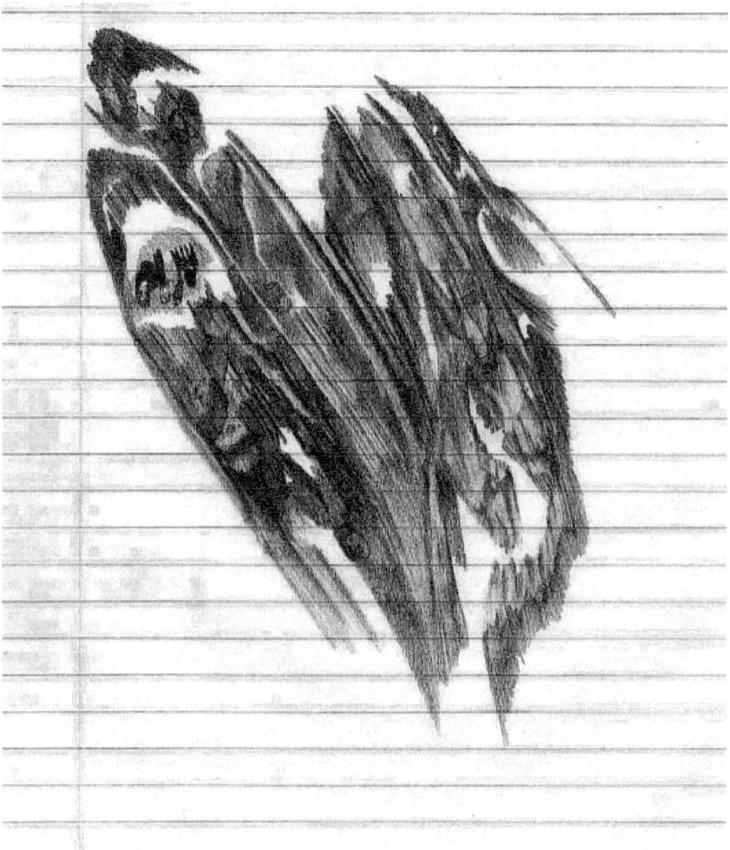

The Hermit

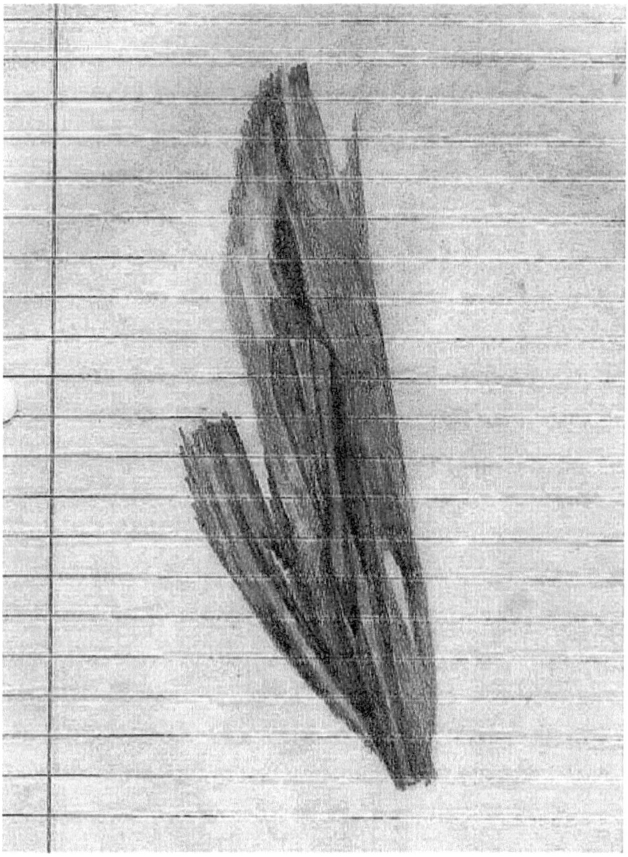

The Mistress of War

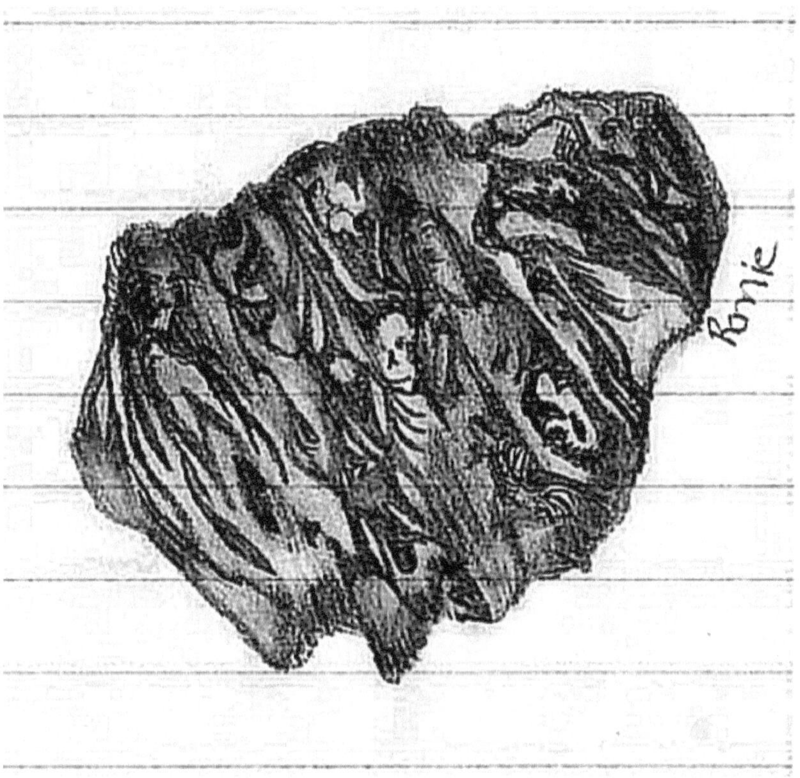
Ronnie

Delusions

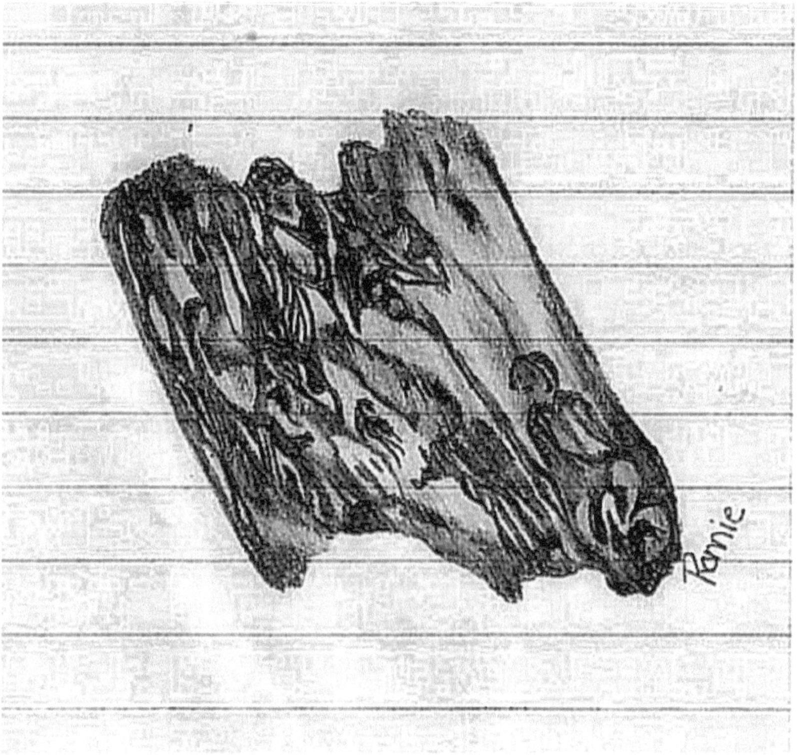
Ronnie

The Arcane

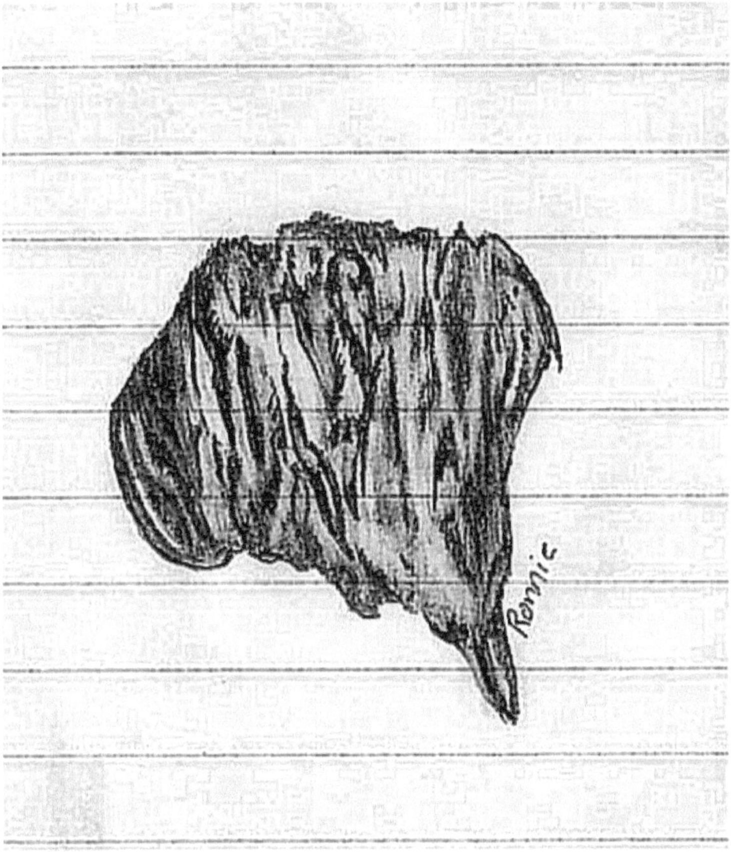
Ronnie

Secrets

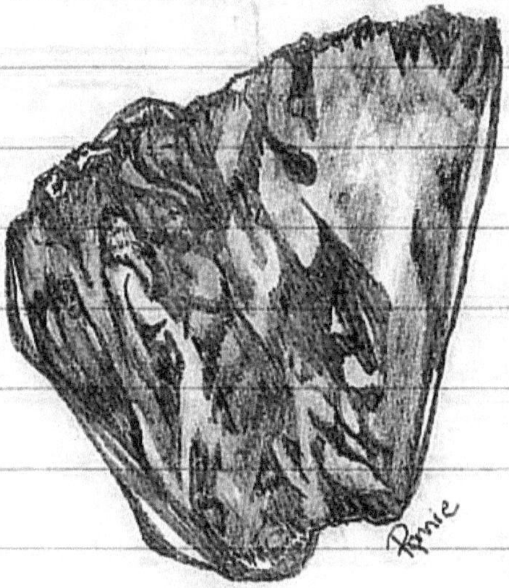

Faces in Shadow

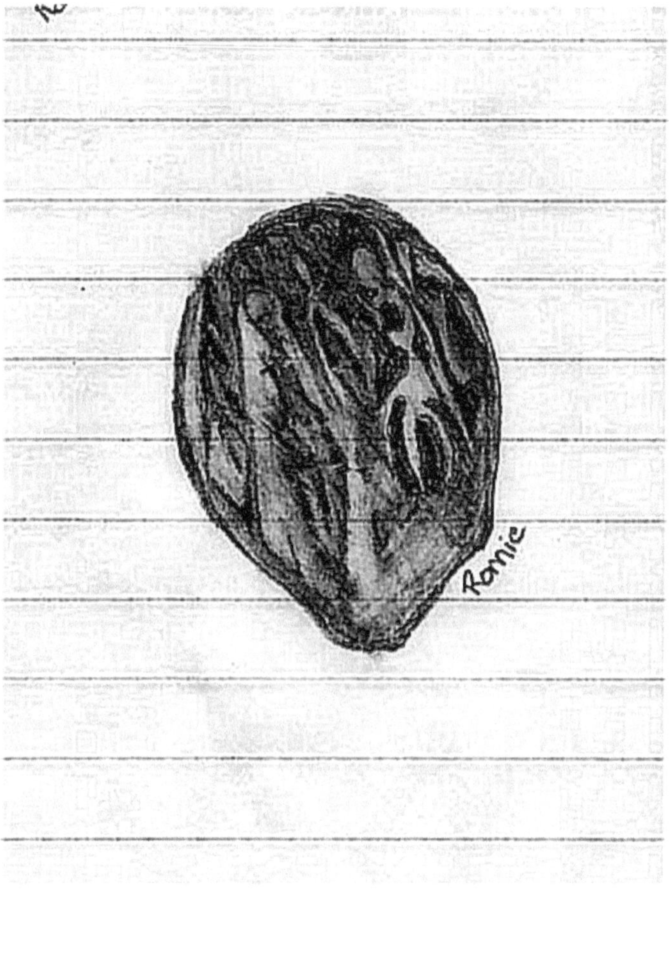
Ronnie

The Stare

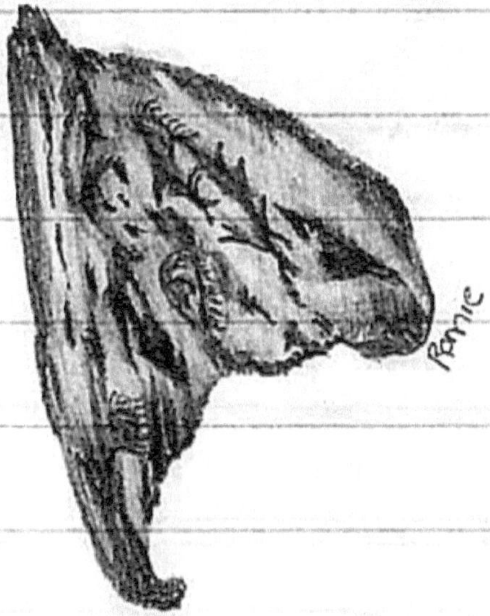

Man And Ghost

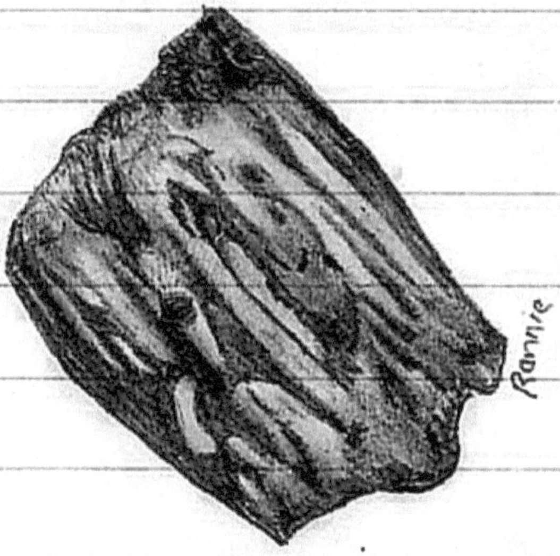
Rannie

Clown Face

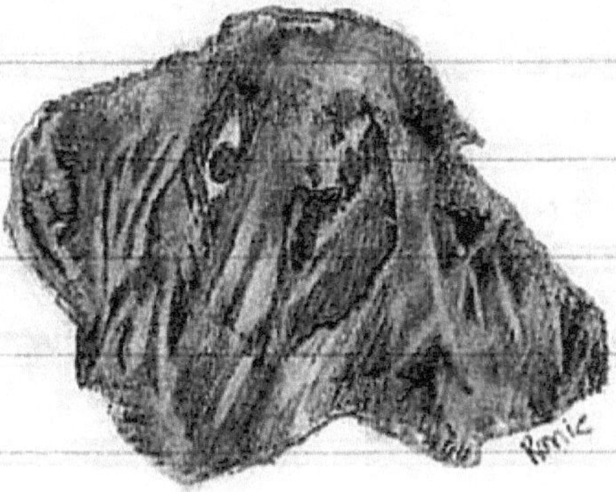

The Dog

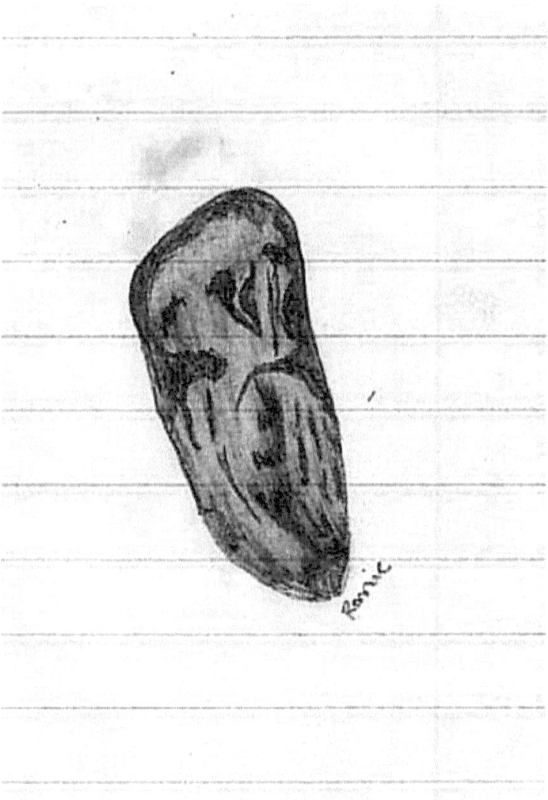

The Face

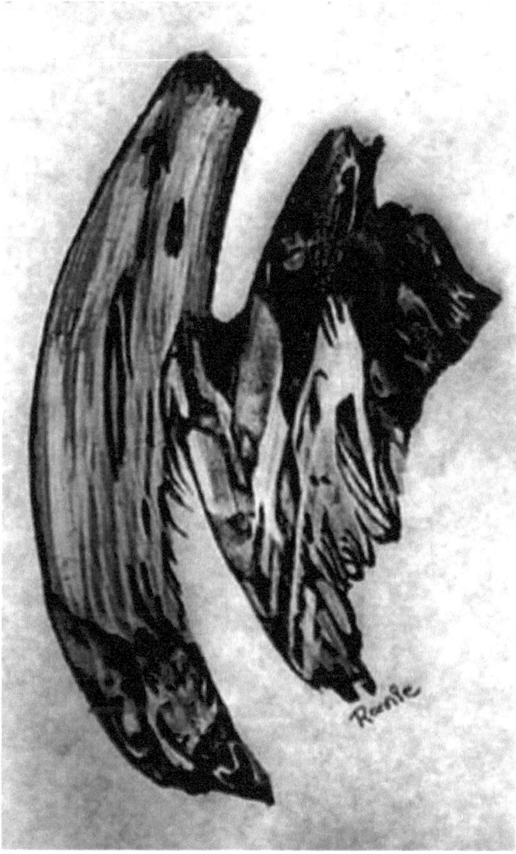
Ronnie

The Face

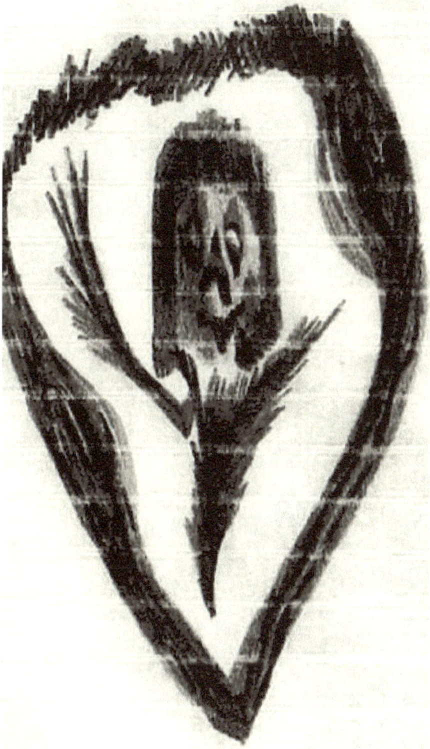

The Heart

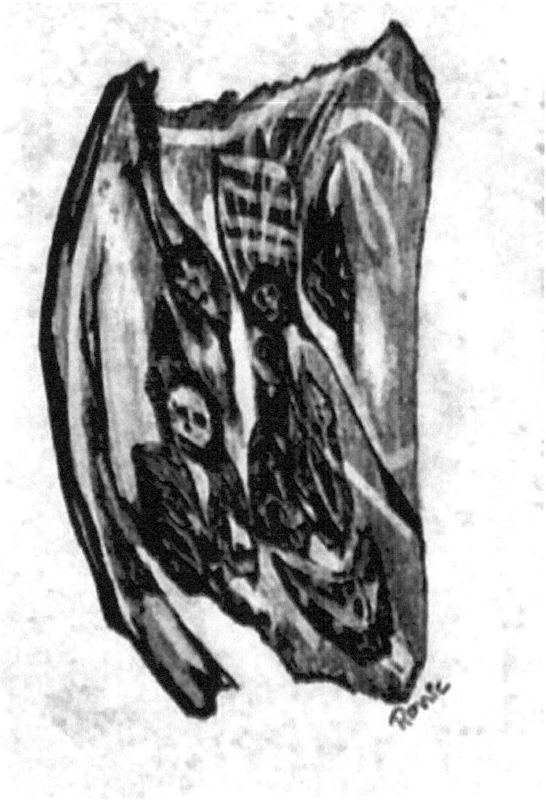
Ronit

Shadows

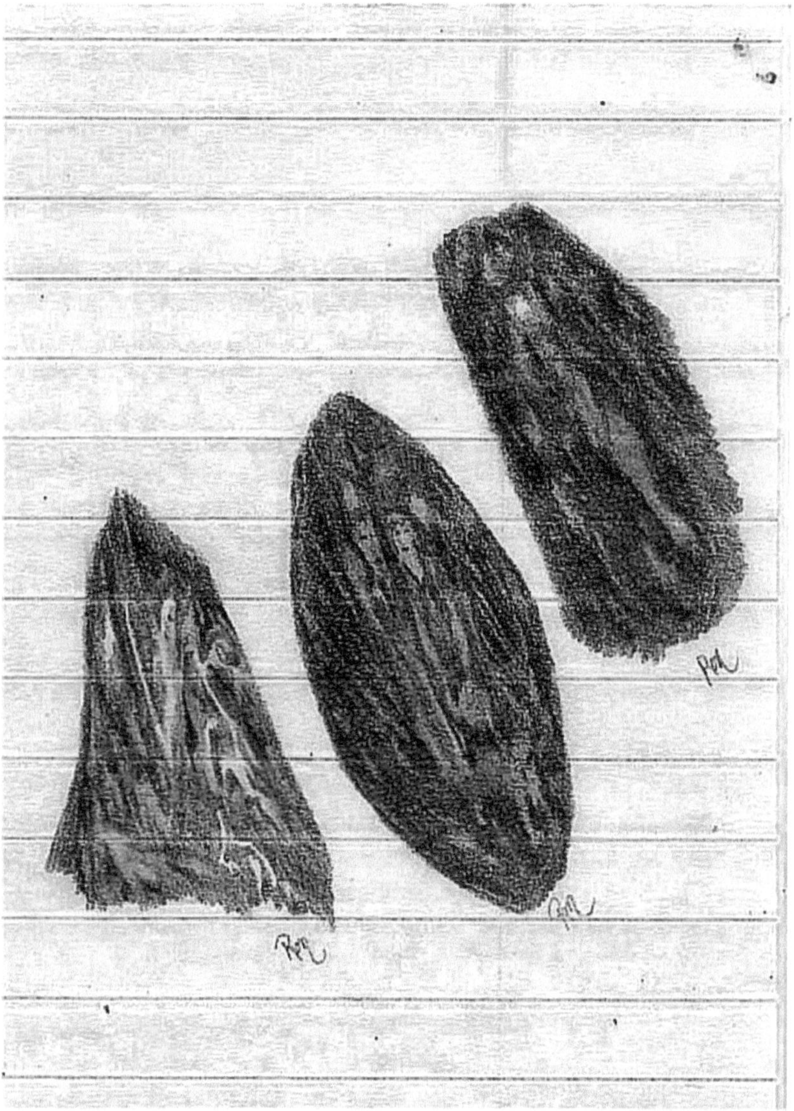

Three Maidens

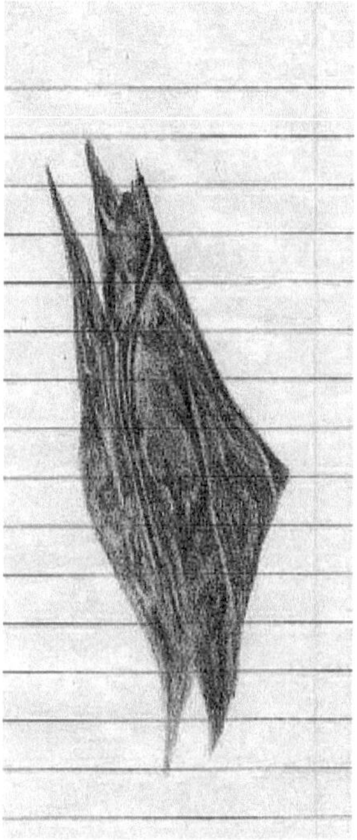

Surreal Secret

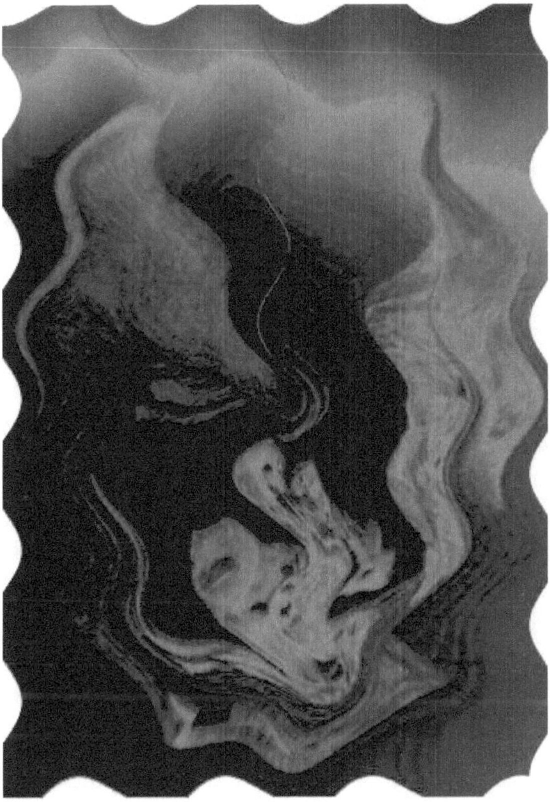

She Dreams

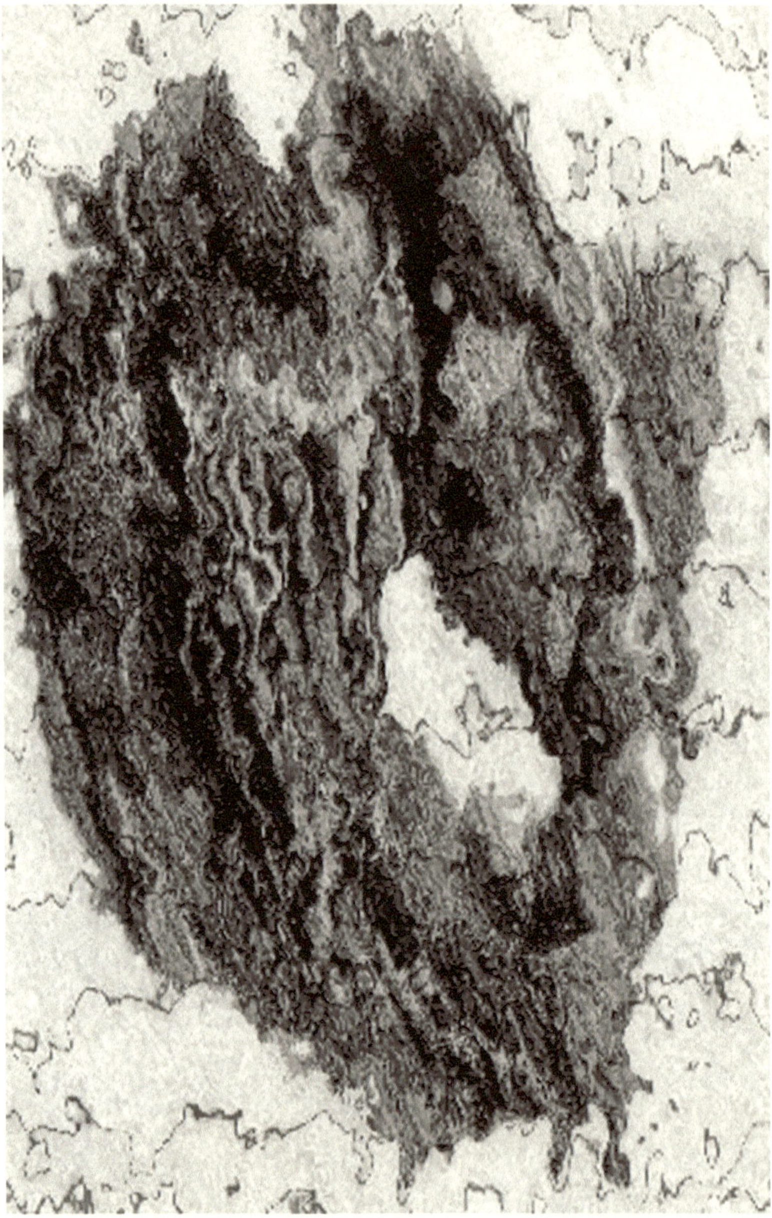

Prayers In Limbo

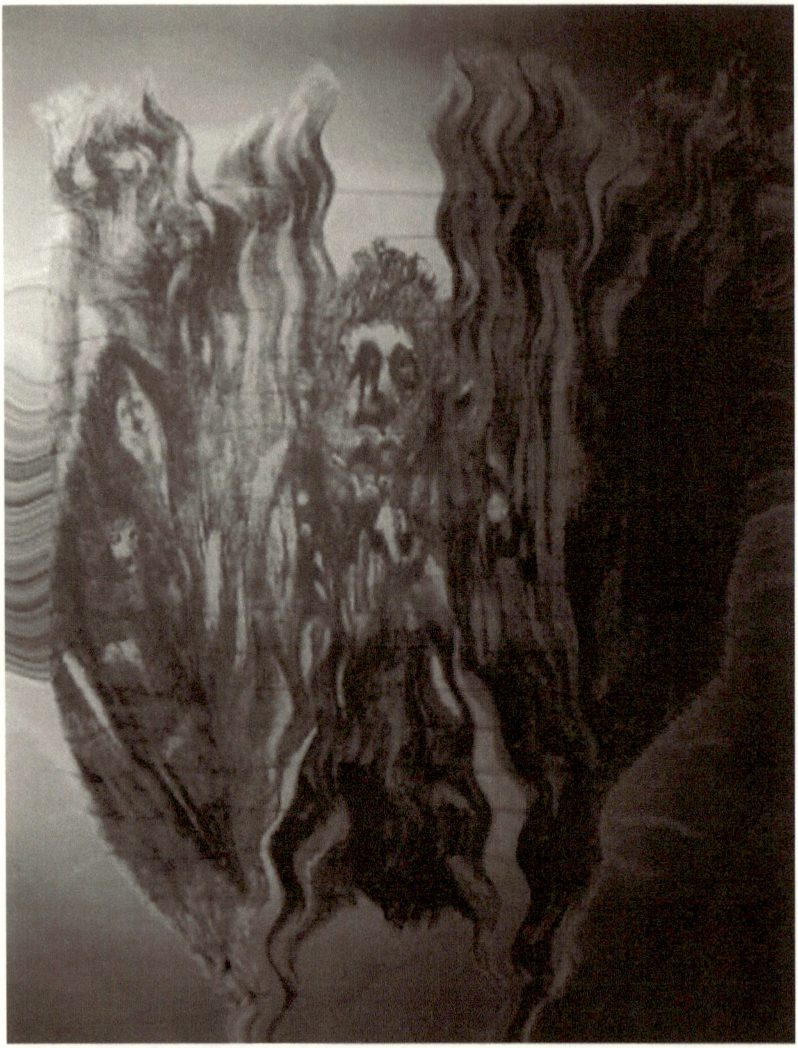

The Tears of A Butterfly In Sorrow

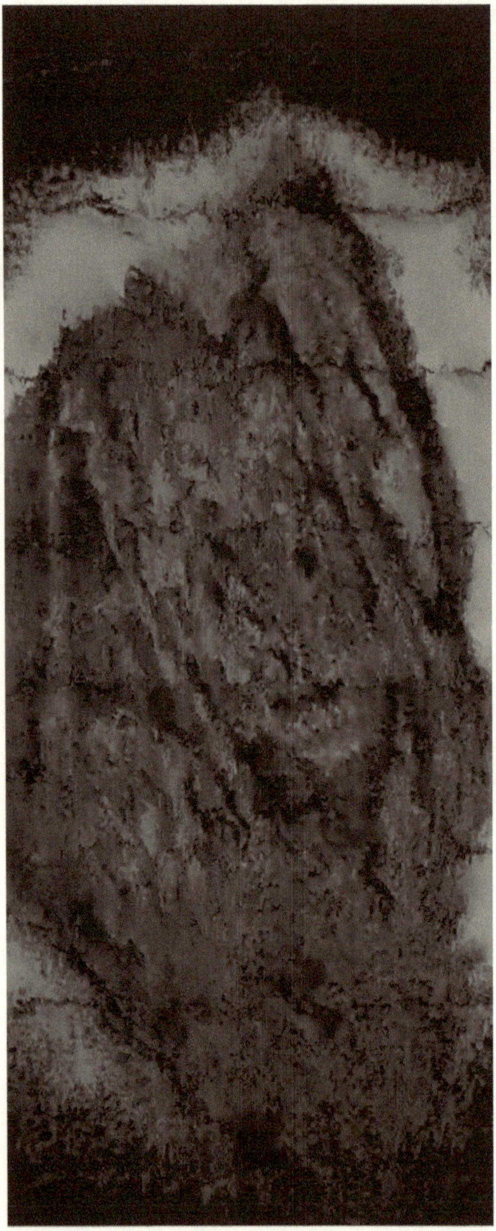

Escape to Avalon

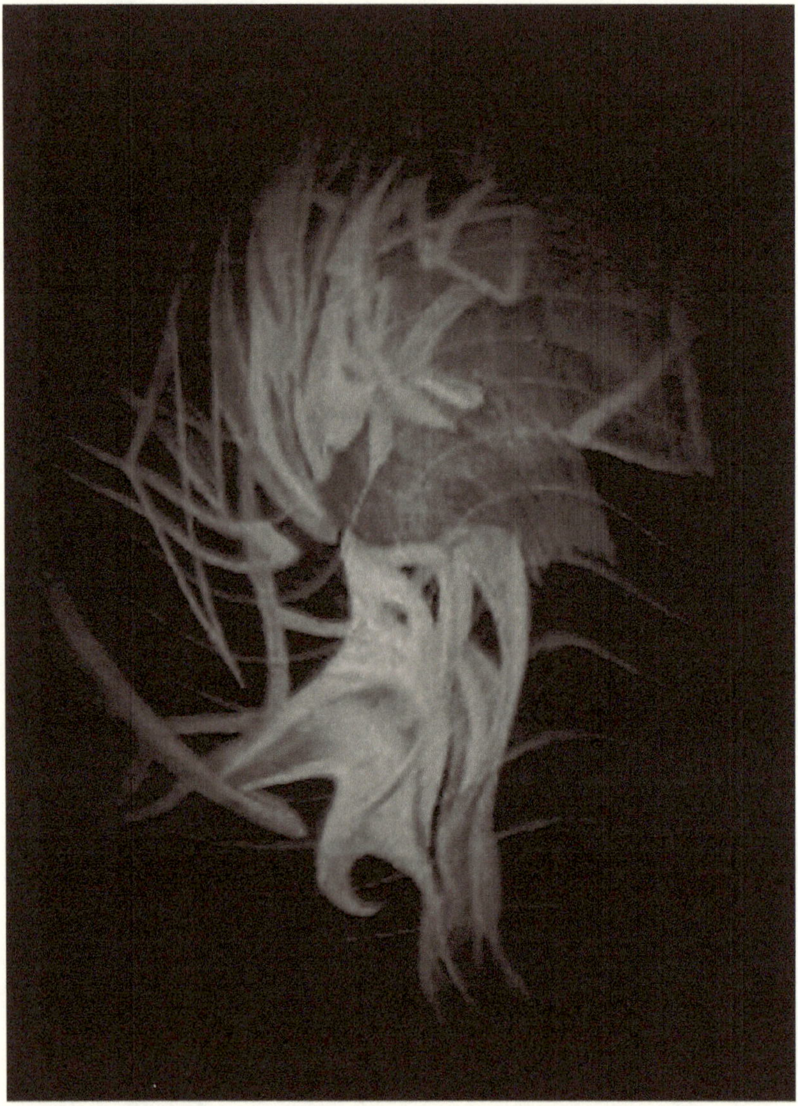

Angles In Red

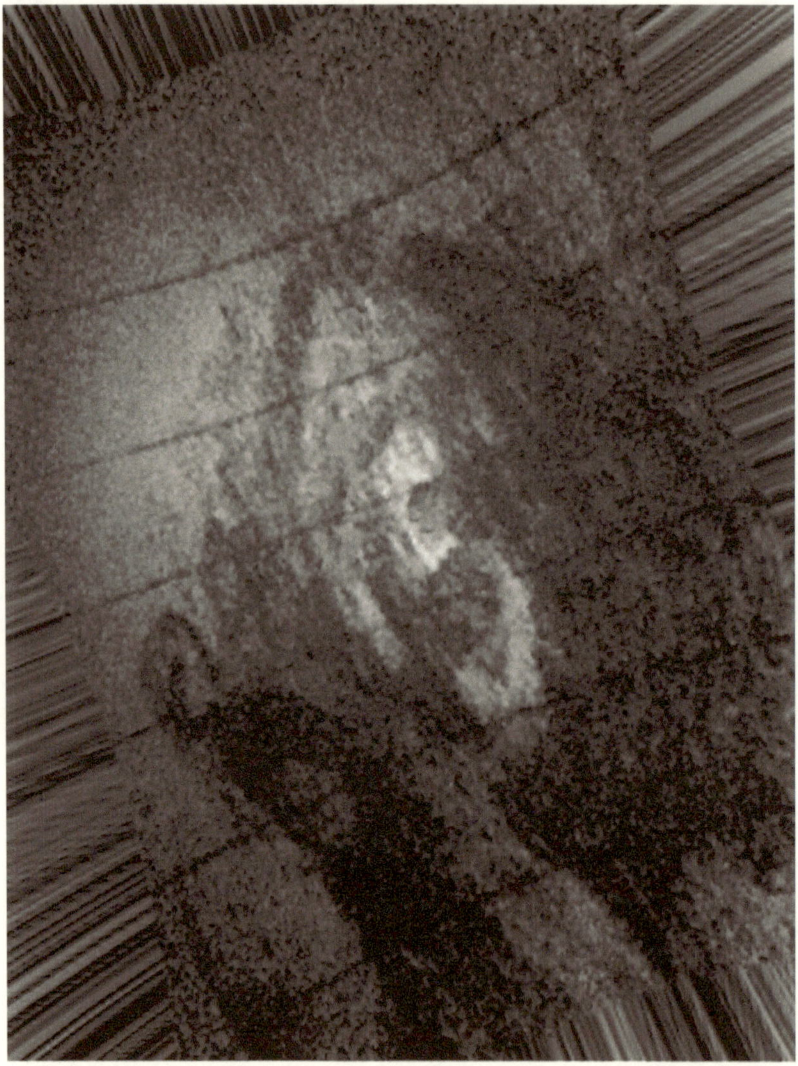

Woman In Misery and Contemplation

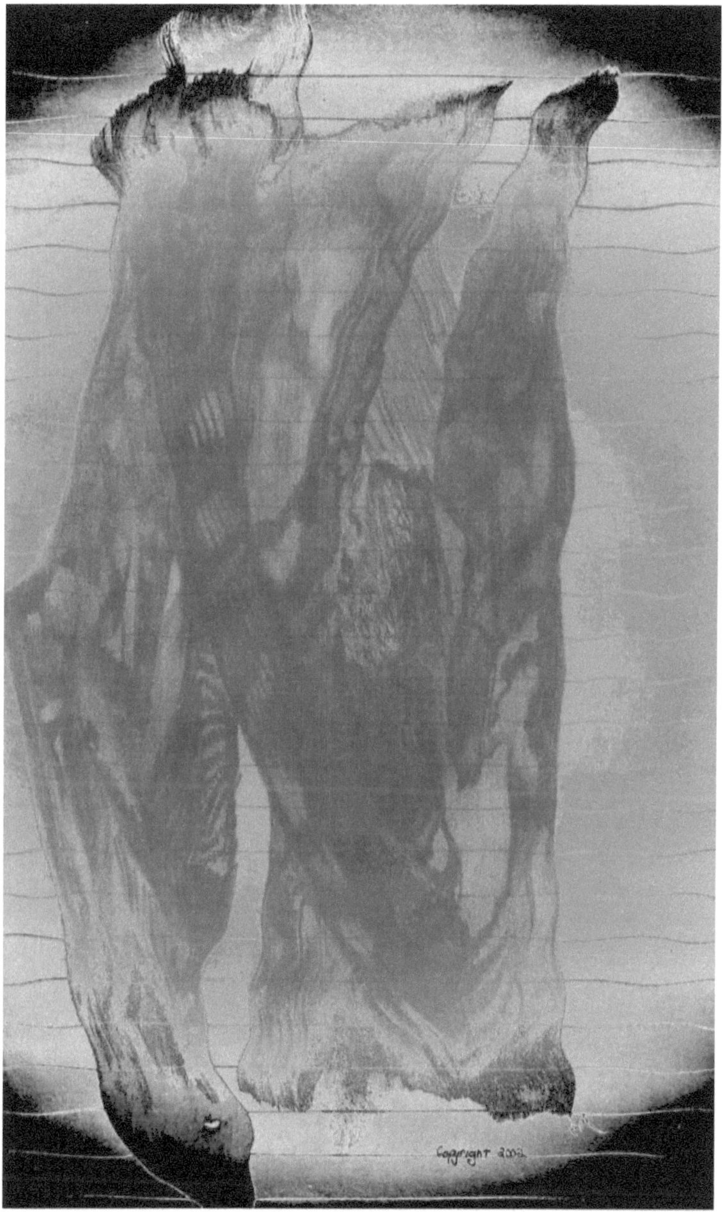
Copyright 2002

Butterfly 2

Thank you for your Attention!!!

www.ingramcontent.com/pod-product-compliance
Lightning Source LLC
Chambersburg PA
CBHW031835170526
45157CB00001B/308
* 9 7 8 1 4 8 2 5 2 1 4 3 6 *